ÖSTERREICHISCHE AKADEMIE DER WISSENSCHAFTEN
PHILOSOPHISCH-HISTORISCHE KLASSE
SITZUNGSBERICHTE, 819. BAND

VERÖFFENTLICHUNGEN ZUR IRANISTIK
HERAUSGEGEBEN VON BERT G. FRAGNER UND VELIZAR SADOVSKI

NR. 61

YURI STOYANOV

DEFENDERS AND ENEMIES OF THE TRUE CROSS

The Sasanian Conquest of Jerusalem in 614 and Byzantine Ideology of Anti-Persian Warfare

Verlag der
Österreichischen Akademie
der Wissenschaften

Wien 2011

Vorgelegt von w. M. BERT G. FRAGNER
in der Sitzung am 1. Oktober 2010

British Library Cataloguing in Publication data
A Catalogue record of this book is available from the British Library

Die verwendete Papiersorte ist aus chlorfrei gebleichtem Zellstoff hergestellt,
frei von säurebildenden Bestandteilen und alterungsbeständig.

ISBN 978-3-7001-6957-4

Druck: Ferdinand Berger & Söhne Ges.m.b.H., A-3580 Horn

Printed and bound in the EU

http://hw.oeaw.ac.at/6957-4
http://verlag.oeaw.ac.at

TABLE OF CONTENTS

INTRODUCTION

The role of the last Sasanian Persian-East Roman/Byzantine war (603-628), customarily seen as the last great war of antiquity, in setting the stage for the sweeping political, religious, social and cultural transformations which by the end of the seventh century affected most of the Eastern Mediterranean and Near East cannot be overestimated. The various political, military, religious and cultural facets of the war continue to attract intense scholarly attention and periodic reassessments[1] triggered by reevaluations of the provenance and textual history of the written sources for the war and the expanding investigation of the archaeology of seventh century Asia Minor, Transcaucasia, Syria, Palestine and Egypt where most of military operations took place.

The written sources for the war (on a number of occasions supported by archaeological evidence) allow for the reconstruction of its general course and phases, although inevitable uncertainties and obscurities surround various details, localities and sub-stages of a military conflict which was extensive both in scope and time. Taking advantage of the political instability in Constantinople in the wake of the dethronement and execution of Maurice in 602 (who had helped him to regain his throne), the Sasanian ruler Xusraw II Parwez (590-628) exploited the imperial *coup d'état* as a fitting *casus belli* and intervened militarily in the subsequent political struggles. His intervention was to evolve eventually into a large-scale invasion of imperial territory, encroaching upon Byzantine Syria, Palestine, Egypt and Anatolia. The enthronement of Heraclius (610-641), son of the *exarchos* of Carthage, as a new emperor, following another *coup d'état* that

---

1 For earlier studies of the conflict, see, for example, Gerland 1894; Baynes 1904; Pernice 1905; Baynes 1912; Baynes 1912a; Baynes 1912-1913; Christensen 1936:447-450; Frolow 1953; Ostrogorsky 1957:92-106; for more recent studies and summaries of the war cf. Stratos 1968:56-66, 103-117, 135-234; Oikonomidès 1971; Pertusi 1971; Oikonomidès 1975; Stratos 1979; Cameron 1979; Altheim-Stiehl 1992; Flusin 1992:2:67-93, 129-181; Haldon 1990:32-34, 41-47; Howard-Johnston 1994; Carile 1994:47-68; Howard-Johnston 1995; Frendo 1995; Howard-Johnston 1996; Haldon: 1999:19-21; Carile 2000; Frendo 2000; Russell 2001; Howard-Johnston 2002; Zuckerman 2002; Kaegi 2003: chs. 2-5; Foss 2003; Howard-Johnston 2004; Shahîd 2004; Sivan 2004; Howard-Johnston 2006; Dignas – Winter 2007:115-119; Mitchell 2007:410-416; Gariboldi 2009; Luttwak 2009:393-409; Ekkebus 2009; Howard-Johnston 2010:ch.14.1, 436-445. A valuable selection of translated extracts from relevant primary sources can be found in Greatrex – Lieu 2002:182-238.

brought down the usurper Phocas (602-610) initially failed to turn the tide of the Persian invasion: after conquering Damascus in 613 and Jerusalem in 614, the Sasanian troops pressed on with the occupation of Egypt between 616 and 621. Advancing through Asia Minor the Persian forces eventually approached the Bosphorus, setting the stage for a direct frontal assault on Constantinople, a threat made all the more dangerous as it was planned in alliance with the Turkic Avar khaganate. The Avar power base lay to the north of the Danube, but concurrent with the Persian advance Avar forces had been pursuing far-ranging incursions across the imperial Danube frontier and deep into the Balkans towards Constantinople.

These plans for a joint attack on and siege of Constantinople, however, proved abortive, and the complete fiasco of a Persian-Avaro-Slav military offensive against the imperial capital in 626 resulted not only in the withdrawal of Persian and Avar forces, but also signaled a turning point in the long war. By that time Heraclius' increasingly effective tactic of outmanoeuvring Persian armies in Asia Minor and (with the crucial assistance of the forces of his ally, the Western Turkic Khaganate) Transcaucasia, as well as expanding his campaigns deep into Sasanian territory, was beginning to change the course of war. After defeating a Persian army at Nineveh in late 627 Heraclius began threatening manoeuvres in relatively close proximity to the Sasanian capital Ctesiphon, pillaging the area and the deserted royal castles there. As political turmoil in Persia began to mount, Xusraw II was deposed and executed and amid the ensuing lasting Sasanian dynastic crisis Heraclius was able to procure a victorious truce, providing for the Persian evacuation of the occupied imperial territories and to start negotiations for the exact delineation of the Byzantine-Sasanian frontiers.

The prolonged conflict between Heraclius' and Xusraw's armies represented the concluding violent stages of four centuries of political and military rivalry that erupted periodically into bitter hostilities between the Sasanian and Roman, and later, the East Roman and Byzantine empires. This inter-imperial rivalry had a characteristic religious dimension which was to be come more prominent during the exhausting and wide-scale Byzantine-Sasanian wars between 603 and 628. Following the Persian invasion of Byzantine Palestine in 614 Christian communities in the Byzantine empire and its Persian-occupied territories found themselves the recipient of disturbing news and circulating stories of the Persian seizure and sack of Jerusalem in May of the same year, alongside reports of the apparent desecration and burning of churches and monasteries within and around the Holy City, including the Holy Sepulchre itself. Apart from the deportation of large groups of Jerusalem Christians, led by the Jerusalem Patriarch Zachariah to Ctesiphon, the Persian expatriation of church treasures and relics to the Sasanian capital, including the reliquary of the "True Cross" on which Jesus was supposed to have been crucified and whose discovery was commonly attributed to St. Helena (and by then associated by Christians and non-Christians alike with Roman Christian imperial victory ideology), were inevitably highly traumatic for Christian sensitivities.

The Persian capture of Jerusalem and the reported destruction and profanation of its paradigmatic Christian shrines was seen in contemporaneous (especially Byzantine) Christendom as an unparalleled calamity, provoking much soul-searching as the devastation of the "Holy Places of Christ" needed to be accounted for within some kind of Christian providential framework and salvation plan of history. Late Roman Christian reactions to natural and political cataclysms or military defeats were commonly based on a theodicy which attributed these adversities to divine punishment of the depravity or fatal flaws of the particular emperor during whose reign they occurred, or of the sins of the citizens of the empire who could not always live up to the elevated ideal of the Christian Roman empire as the "new Israel". Amid the spiritual turmoil provoked by the fall of Jerusalem, the "Holy City of Christ", the calamity could be blamed on the sins of its inhabitants generating contamination which could be "purified" only by the fire and sword of the invading Persians.[2] The imperial political and ecclesiastical elites must have been aware and apprehensive of Christian reactions which predictably could lay the blame for the calamity on some kind of culpable breaches and transgressions of Christian norms and piety at their highest levels.[3]

---

2 Strategios, *Expugnatio* (Arabic version C), 6:9-11 (ed. Garitte 1974: vol. 2, t. 26, 120; Lat. transl. Garitte 1974: vol. 2, t. 27, 80).

3 See, for example, the summary of contemporaneous Christian reactions of the fall of Byzantine Jerusalem to the Sasanian army in Kaegi 2003:78-80. Cf. Wheeler 1991:77-80, 83-85; Wilken 1992:216-233; Olster 1998:79-84; Stemberger 1999:261-64.

Christian attitudes to and interpretations of the Persian conquest of Jerusalem could also fall back on the rhetorical strategies of Christian biblical typology as developed in the various genres of Byzantine literature, which viewed the fortunes of the empire and its imperial and ecclesiastical figures through the prism of paradigmatic Old Testament events and their protagonists. Christian Jerusalem could be thus re-discovered as the navel of the earth (Ezekiel 5:5), its Persian capture seen as the realization of the divine punishment to be unleashed on the city on account of its "abominations" pronounced in Ezekiel 16, whereas the travails of its Christian inhabitants could be depicted as being presaged by Israel's Babylonian captivity and bondage in Egypt.[4]

The Byzantine counter-offensive in Sasanian-controlled territory resorted to some (ostensibly retaliatory) destruction of Sasanian secular and religious complexes, including one of the three principal fire temples of Sasanian Zoroastrianism, Adur-Gusnasp, at Takht-e Soleyman in north-western Iran.[5] Byzantine campaigning was also accompanied by sustained anti-Sasanian religio-political propaganda targeting (particularly in Transcaucasia) the Christian subjects of the Persian state. Following the successful conclusion of the war in 628, the recovery of Jerusalem and the Holy Land was naturally to be seen in Byzantium as a sign of divine forgiveness and another indication of the divinely-ordained destiny of the "New Israel," following on and confirming the trajectory of the anticipated restoration of Christian imperial order. After its negotiated restitution, along with other church relics abducted from Jerusalem, the True Cross was restored to the Holy City and reinstalled in the Church of Holy Sepulchre by Heraclius (reportedly in March 630) in what appear to have been carefully staged solemnities, replete with symbolic and ideological significance. The rescue and exaltation of other sacred relics from the Holy Land such as the Holy Sponge and Holy Lance had already been staged at an earlier period of the war in Constantinople, while Heraclius himself had undertaken a triumphant return to the imperial city during which, for the first time in the history of the Christian Roman empire, liturgical procedures were incorporated into the

---

4 For articulations of these notions, see Sophronios, *Anacreontica*, 14, 20 (ed. Gigante 1957:102-107, 123-128); Strategios, *Expugnatio* (Arabic version C), 18:8-11 (ed. Garitte 1974:vol. 2, t. 26, 135; Lat. transl. Garitte 1974:vol. 2, t. 27, 91).

5 Nikephoros, *Breviarum Historicum*, 12:41-43 (ed. Mango 1990:55); George of Pisidia, *Heraclias*, 2.167-230.

traditional victory parades.[6] This sequence of ceremonial displays showed that the warrior-emperor and his court publicists intended to fortify and embellish his growing stature as a defender of Christendom and vehicle of divine will and salvation, as Heraclius' restitution of the True Cross clearly marked the symbolic climax of his Persian campaigns, portrayed as a victory for Roman/Byzantine Christianity. Heraclius' famed *restitutio crucis*, which later both in Eastern and Western Christendom was to be seen as the high point of his reign, appears also to have been the vital element of a religio-political programme underpinned by the evolving synthesis of late Roman/Byzantine eschatology and imperial ideology.

The purpose of this monograph is to explore the roots of some of the crucial elements of this religio-political programme which were concepttualized in reaction to the Persian conquest of Jerusalem in 614 and its repercussions for Byzantine political theology and Christian ideology of warfare.[7]

---

6 See the analysis of the incorporation of liturgical processions in Heraclius' victory celebrations in Constantinople in McCormick 1986:70-73, 391-92.

7 I acknowledge with gratitude that this monograph was written with the support (and within a research project) of the Peace Research Institute (PRIO), Oslo, Norway.

CHAPTER 1

THE ARCHAEOLOGY OF THE PERSIAN CONQUEST OF JERUSALEM IN 614 AND THE WRITTEN SOURCES

The Sasanian conquest of Palestine and Jerusalem in 614 by the forces of the Persian army commander, Šāhwarāz, was undoubtedly one of the most momentous events of the second phase of the last East Roman/Byzantine-Persian war. It dealt a severe blow to Byzantine military and religious morale, which was perturbed to its core by the phenomenon of the Christian Roman debacle in the Holy Land and Holy City, while further boosting the growing self-confidence of the Sasanian political/military elite and of Xusraw II who in 615 spurned Heraclius' renewed overtures to negotiate a peaceful settlement.[8] The extant sources make it possible to generally reconstruct the routes of the Sasanian invasion of Palestine along with what was portrayed as the devastating siege and seizure of Jerusalem.[9] While differing in some details and in their chronology of events, the Christian sources for the Sasanian capture of Jerusalem[10] build a combined picture of

[8] Theophanes *Chronographia* AM 6109 (ed. de Boor 1883:301:20-25).

[9] For more recent re-assessments of the course of the Sasanian invasion, cf. Avi-Yonah 1984:258-264; Schick 1995:20-26 (with a critical analysis of the archaeological evidence); Kaegi 2003:77-78; Greatrex – Lieu 2002:190-191.

[10] No contemporaneous Sasanian sources of the Persian capture of Jerusalem have been preserved. The seventh-century Christian sources include the 'treatise' on the Persian capture of Jerusalem by the Mar Saba monk, Strategios, extant in Georgian and Arab versions as well as Greek fragments (ed. Garitte 1960, 1973-1974), anacreontic poems by Sophronios, a monk of the St Theodosius monastery and would-be Patriarch of Jerusalem (ed. Gigante 1957); the anonymous *Chronicon paschale* (ed. Dindorf 1832); the *Life of St George of Choziba* (ed. House 1888); the *Life of St John the Almsgiver* (ed. Delehaye 1927) the Armenian chronicle attributed to Sebeos, Bishop of the Bagratouni (ed. Abgarian 1979, English transl.: Thomson–Howard-Johnston–Greenwood 1999); the anonymous East Syrian *Khuzistan Chronicle* (ed. Guidi 1903). Later sources alluding to or providing further details about the events surrounding the Sasanian takeover and occupation of Jerusalem include Theophanes' *Chronographia* (ed. de Boor 1883-1885) and the universal chronicles of Eutychius of Alexandria (ed. Breydy 1985) and Michael the Syrian (ed. Chabot 1899-1910) as well as al-Ṭabarī's *History of the Prophets and Kings* (vol. 5, transl. Bosworth 1999). There are substantial differences between the accounts of Strategios and Sebeos in their treatment of the events leading to the Persian siege and storming of Jerusalem. According to Strategius, the Persian army commanders

the massive Persian destruction of churches and monasteries in Jerusalem and its environs, indiscriminate massacres of the Christian population (clerics, monks and civilians) and the deportation of large groups of Christian survivors, led by the Jerusalem Patriarch Zachariah to Ctesiphon. Among these accounts, the sermon on the Persian capture of Jerusalem ascribed to the Mar Saba monk Strategios (a composite text comprising narratives belonging to different genres and dates between the Persian capture of Jerusalem in 614 and Heraclius' *restitutio crucis* sixteen years later)[11] includes a grueling and graphic account of anti-Christian violence perpetrated by the Persian invaders and their Jewish allies.[12] Yet the ever-growing archaeological record indicates that the actual impact of the Sasanian invasion was rather negligible[13] making the critical scrutiny of the striking discrepancies between the written and archaeological evidence all the more important for reconstructing and interpreting at least some crucial

---

proposed a treaty with the city's inhabitants arranging for its peaceful takeover (as in the case of the great majority of similar urban areas in Palestine which accepted Sasanian sovereignty without violence) and such a treaty would have been welcomed by the Jerusalem Patriarch Zacharias but it was rejected by the representatives of the traditionally riotous circus factions in Jerusalem who in this manner are blamed for triggering the calamity of Persian siege and onslaught (Strategios, *La prise*, 5.7-11; Strategios, *Expugnatio,* 5.7-11). According to Sebeos 114-115, Jerusalem at first actually surrendered peacefully to the Persian army commanders and an apparently small Persian military force took charge of the city; its members were, however, killed in a subsequent Christian rebellion which also provoked massive Jewish-Christian inter-communal violence, leading to a great loss of life among the Jewish inhabitants – in this version the Persian siege was a response to the massacre of its military representatives and the severe Jewish-Christian violence in the city.

11 Strategios, *La prise* (ed. Garitte 1960); Strategios, *Expugnatio* (ed. Garitte 1973-1974); on Strategios' sermon, its versions and the historicity of its narratives concerning the Persian capture of Jerusalem, see, for example, Couret 1897; Clermont-Ganneau 1898; Conybeare 1910 (along with a partial English translation of the Georgian version); Cerulli 1946; Peeters 1951; Milik 1961; Baras 1982:302-304; Wheeler 1991:77-80, 83-85; Wilken 1992:218-224; Flusin 1992:2, 159-161; Speck 1997b; Dauphin 1998:2,352-60 *passim*; Olster 1998:79-84; Stemberger 1999:261-63; Cameron 2002:61-62; Howard-Johnston 2004:102; Jacobs 2004:196-199. On the composite nature of the sermon and for the dates of its component narratives, see now Howard-Johnston 2010:ch. 6.1, 163-171; ch13.1, 420-423 (I wish to express my gratitude to Howard-Johnston for making available to me the pre-publication proofs of the first six chapters of his book in advance of its publication in 2010).

12 For the Christian accounts of Jewish involvement in supposed anti-Christian atrocities in Jerusalem, see ch. 3, n. 8 below.

13 Cf. Schick 1995:20-26; Maeir 2000; Russell 2001:44-47; Avni 2010.

facets of the historical reality of the Persian conquest and occupation of Jerusalem and the Holy Land.

The seventh-century Christian sources for the Persian conquest of Jerusalem allege that the city suffered major devastation after its fall to the Sasanian armies and that much of it was set on fire, with churches, in particular, becoming the target of wanton burning and destruction during what Strategios describes as a merciless sack of the city[14] in which Jewish allies of the invaders also took an active part. These accounts, however, lament the destruction of Jerusalem's sacral architecture in general and without offering much concrete details; the *Khuzistan Chronicle* and *Chronicon Paschale* state in addition that the Church of the Holy Sepulchre was set on fire,[15] while Strategios' sermon asserts that both the Church of the Holy Sepulchre and the Church of Holy Zion were set aflame[16] and lists also a number of Jerusalem church locations where numerous Christians were supposed to have lost their lives.[17] The later chronicle of Eutychius of Alexandria asserts that apart from setting ablaze the Church of the Holy Sepulchre, the Sasanian forces destroyed the Church of Gethsemane and the Eleona Church on the Mount of Olives.[18]

Despite the discrepancies between their narratives, their manifest (and inevitable) wartime and religiously-motivated polemical bias, propagandizing overtones and forceful anti-Persian and anti-Jewish stereotyping (including the use of the standard *topoi* of East Roman/Byzantine anti-Sasanian and anti-Jewish polemic), the veracity of these written accounts of the Persian capture of Jerusalem has been and continues to be accepted uncritically in a number of historical and archaeological publications dealing with various aspects of the political, social and religious history of the Near East and the Eastern Mediterranean

---

14 Cf. Strategios, *La prise,* 8.7-26; Strategios, *Expugnatio,* 8.7-22; Sophronios, *Anacreontica* 14.69-102; *Life of St John the Almsgiver*, 9; *Chronicon Paschale,* 704; *Khuzistan Chronicle,* 27.

15 *Chronicon Paschale,* 704; *Khuzistan Chronicle,* 27.

16 Strategios, *Expugnatio* 11.7 (Arabic version A); Strategios, *La prise,* 11.7, 13.15.

17 Strategios, *La prise,* 23; for assessments of these church locations and the death-toll alleged in the different versions of the sermon, see Milik 1961; Flusin 1992:II, 159-161; Schick 1995:34-37.

18 Eutychius, *Annalen*, 119.

in the seventh century, as well as in general histories of the region during late antiquity and the early Middle Ages. Although Jerusalem was one of the very few places to be taken by force during the Sasanian invasion and occupation of Palestine, the written sources' narratives of violent takeover, the systematic destruction of Christendom's most holy places and the massive slaughter of both ecclesiastic and lay Christians in Jerusalem have been often projected over the whole of the Sasanian-occupied Holy Land. The Sasanian invasion and brief period of occupation of Byzantine Palestine have been accordingly regularly seen as having an a calamitous effect on Christianity in the Holy Land and its ecclesiastical order and sacral architecture, severely undermining the ability of the Christian communities to maintain or revive their religious observance and worship during the period of Sasanian suzerainty following the envisaged violence and disorder of the Persian offensive.

In this line of argument, the re-assertion of Byzantine authority in its Sasanian-occupied provinces following Heraclius' victorious truce with the post-Xusraw Sasanian regime in 628 was too ephemeral to secure a proper recovery for Christianity in the Holy Land. The wide-scale destruction of Christian sacral architecture and the very structures of Christian life in Jerusalem as narrated in contemporaneous Christian narratives have been hence seen as having a wide-spread effect on other Christian centres and communities in Palestine.[19] In this view the Persian invasion and occupation of Palestine can be seen as not only causing wide-spread economic decline and social breakdown,[20] but also disrupting the rhythm and functioning of Christian religious life in the region, anticipating the subsequent major political and religious challenges posed by the Moslem Arab conquests in Palestine in the 630s which local Christianity encountered greatly weakened on all levels.

In a wider sphere, a number of historians have interpreted the Persian conquest of Byzantine Palestine as one of the crucial episodes of the massive political, socio-economic and religious transformation of the Near East that began in the seventh-century, initiated by the Persian conquests which were

---

19 See, for example, Mayerson 1964:191-192; Ovadiah 1970:218 (specifically on Jerusalem, 76, 82, 90).

20 See, for example, Stratos 1968:109-111; 258-259; Tsafrir – Foerster 1997:145.

seen as effectively marking the end of antiquity.[21] Accordingly, the Sasanian early seventh-century conquests in Byzantine Asia Minor, Syria, Palestine and Egypt have been regularly credited with the destruction and depopulation of urban centres and settlements, the decline of agriculture and trade in the Eastern Mediterranean and the undermining of the Graeco-Roman civilizational and cultural hegemony (in its Christian East Roman version) in the region, setting thus the stage for the Muslim Arab conquests which dealt it the final, mortal blows.[22]

However, the steady progress of archaeological work in the Eastern Mediterranean and Near East since the nineteenth century has been accompanied by a growing awareness that the veracity of the written sources regarding many of the political, religious and cultural transformations and developments in the region during late antiquity and the early Middle Ages need to be constantly re-evaluated against the background of the archaeological evidence, already existing or newly made available. This holds particular relevance with regard to the existing (and often contradictory) documentary sources for the political and religious history of ancient and medieval Jerusalem and its environs where the expansion of archaeological investigation (which began in the nineteenth century and assumed a systematic and professional nature following the establishment of the British Mandate in Palestine after World War I) has been constantly triggering re-assessments of these written records.

On the other hand, not a few archaeological investigations and publications have tended to accept the lead and general truthfulness of the written records regarding the Sasanian conquest of Byzantine Palestine, and on a number of occasions evidence of destruction and the presence of ash layers (but without the necessary supporting pottery and numismatic data or presence of Sasanian artifacts) at the relevant urban, rural and especially church locations have been ascribed to the Persian invasion. This tendency, which has attracted some sustained criticism,[23] can be traced largely to

---

21 See, for example, Kondakov 1904:173-174; Vasiliev 1952:195-196; Foss:1975.

22 See the summary of these approaches to the early seventh century Sasanian conquests in the Eastern Mediterranean in Foss 2003:149-151.

23 See Magness:1992; Schick 1995:22-24, 253-255, 291-292, 387-388, 397-398; Russell 2001:43-44; Silberman 2001:614-616; Avni 2010; Magness 2010.

archaeological publications on late antique and early medieval Palestine in general.[24] The numerous problems posed by such first-choice attribution of destruction layers at church sites to the Sasanian invasion (using the written evidence as a lead when other causes for the damage and the dates it was inflicted are equally or more viable) are highlighted by the uncertainties surrounding the reasons for and timing of the fire damage to a group of churches in the coastal area between Tyre and Akko[25] and the abandonment of the Monastery of St. Martyrius at Ma'ale Adumim to the east of Jerusalem.[26]

This tendency has been particularly pronounced in the archaeological and historical treatment of late antique and early medieval Jerusalem, but the sheer accumulation of archaeological work and evidence in and around Jerusalem (especially over the last thirty years), including reassessments of earlier excavation reports, has severely undermined the credibility of the written sources alleging massive destruction and conflagration of Christian sacral architecture (as well as residential areas) in and around the Holy City. Despite this sustained work, no clear evidence of destruction and burnt layers has been unearthed and some of the earlier or more recent attributions of such levels to the Persian conquest have been persuasively disproved.[27] Indeed, so far only one such ash layer (outside the northern wall of the Old City of Jerusalem and situated between Damascus and Herod's gate) has been discovered that can be tentatively attributed to the Persian siege of the Holy City.[28] Claims for evidence of damage and conflagration in the Byzantine levels to the south of the Temple Mount[29] have been similarly refuted by archaeological work demonstrating the continuity of occupation of the relevant residential area throughout the seventh century and beyond.[30] The same continuity of undisrupted settlement applies to other residential

---

24 See, for example, Crowfoot – Fitzgerald 1929:52-55; Prausnitz – Avi-Yonah – Barag 1967; Edelstein-Dauphine 1975; Tzaferis 1975; Holum – Hohlfelder – Vann – Maltese 1988:202-203; Negev 1993.

25 Schick 1995:27-29, 418-419, 452-454; Russell 2001:47-48.

26 Magen – Talgam 1990; Magen 1993; Schick 1995:32; Russell 2001:46-47; Magness 2010.

27 Magness:1992; Magness 2005; Magness 2010; Avni 2010.

28 Magness 2010.

29 Mazar 2003:4-68.

30 Magness 2005; Magness 2010.

areas in the Old City of Jerusalem which would have suffered heavy damage if one takes the written reports of its Persian capture at face value.[31]

The most dramatic discrepancy between documentary sources and the accumulating archeological evidence concerns the dramatic narratives of the large-scale destruction and burning of Christian sacral architecture described in general detail in the written records. These descriptions appeared convincing enough for a long time and a succession of archaeological and historical studies of Jerusalem or general surveys of the area or the period have faithfully relied on, reproduced, or even expanded their claims.[32] The progress of archaeological investigation and assessments of the archaeological reports on excavated ecclesiastical compounds in Jerusalem and its hinterland, however, have demonstrated the lack of definite evidence of substantial damage or traces of burning datable to the period of the Persian conquest at a number of church sites which, according to the written accounts, suffered heavily during the sack, or were destroyed.

In his ground-breaking 1995 historical and archaeological study of the Christian communities in Palestine during the Byzantine-Umayyad transition from the seventh to mid-eighth century Robert Schick asserted (on the basis of the archaeological evidence available to him at that time): "Thus, without the literary sources, one might conclude that the Sasanian conquest did not have much impact on Jerusalem."[33] His careful scrutiny of the archaeological evidence and excavation reports allowed him to identify the very small number of churches and monasteries which suffered or may have suffered damage or destruction during the Sasanian takeover of Jerusalem.[34] Since the publication of Schick's study historians and archaeologists have been far more cautious in their treatment of the early-seventh century period of Sasanian dominion in Palestine and the ambiguity of the related

---

31 See, for example, Avni – Baruch – Weksler-Bdolah 2001; Weksler-Bdolah 2006-2007; Avni 2010.

32 A short but indicative selections of such publications includes Join-Lambert 1958:140-142 (a characteristic uncritical reading of the literary sources which envisages the wholesale destruction of Jerusalem's Christian sacral architecture in 614); Stratos 1968:109-110; Mare 1987:237; Geva 1992:768; Whittow 1996:75-76.

33 Schick 1995:34.

34 Schick 1995:33-48, 325-359; some of his conclusions are reiterated and summarized in Schick 2007:179-181.

archaeological evidence roughly datable to the early seventh century. It is no longer possible to ignore the archaeological record which suggests that the Christian church compounds suffered substantially less damage and destruction during the Sasanian capture and occupation of Jerusalem than the massive devastation elaborated in the literary sources.[35] More recent archaeological work and reconsideration of excavation reports, moreover, have questioned the reliability or even the presence of archaeological data attesting damage and destruction layers datable to the Sasanian conquest even at the last very few ecclesiastical sites in and around Jerusalem where such evidence still seemed credible after Schick's critical reassessment of the archaeological record.

These sites include the Church of Gethesemane (situated on the western slopes of the Mount of Olives) which Euthychius reports to have been destroyed by the Sasanian army along with the other Mount of Olives' Church of Eleona.[36] Euthychius is clearly wrong about the destruction of the Eleona Church[37] and a new assessment of the original report of the excavations undertaken at the Church of Gethesemane finds no definitive evidence for an early seventh century destruction of this church either, but rather indicates the presence of some data attesting its continuous functioning into the early Islamic period.[38] A similar lack of any conclusive archaeological evidence makes it impossible to substantiate the claims that the Church of St. Stephen (located to the north of the Old City of Jerusalem walls) was destroyed during the Sasanian siege,[39] all the more that recent excavations of the Byzantine monastic complexes in this particular area did not discover any layers of destruction but instead tend to demonstrate a

[35] See, for example, Stemberger 1999:262, 271-272n8; Stemberger 2006:316-317. See also the cautious treatment of the Sasanian conquest and sack of Jerusalem in Gil 1996:1-2; Treadgold 2001:89; Cameron 2002:61-62; Kaegi 2003:78-80; Mitchell 2007:412; Louth 2008:227.

[36] Eutychius, *Annalen*, 119.

[37] Schick 1995:350-351.

[38] Avni 2010 assessing Orfali 1924 and reaching different conclusions from Schick 1995:352-353. Cf. Russell 2001:49. On the controversial literary evidence concerning another Mount of Olives church, which reportedly needed repair after 614 (Antiochus monachus, *Epistula*, 1427-1428), the Church of Ascension, see Schick 1995:354-355.

[39] See the conjectured reason for its posited destruction in Schick 1995:35, 342-343; Schick 2007:179.

continuous use well into the early Islamic era.[40] Destruction levels securely datable to the early seventh century have proved likewise elusive at the two sites associated by their investigators with the reportedly destroyed or substantially damaged Monastery of St. George, respectively to the west of the Old City, at Sheikh Bader (Giv'at Ram),[41] and to the south-west of the Old City, at Ketef Hinnom.[42]

Concerning other Jerusalem church compounds, arguments that the New Church of the Theotokos (the famous *Nea Ekklesia*, the only church to be erected in Jerusalem during Justinian's reign in the sixth century) suffered partial damage during the Sasanian conquest[43] (according to one of the destruction theories it was demolished by the Jewish allies of the Sasanians)[44] have been also refuted by recent excavations.[45] The archaeological record at another Jerusalem ecclesiastical site which has been identified as having possibly suffered damage during the Sasanian takeover and undergone subsequent repair,[46] the Church of the Probatica (situated to the north of the Temple Mount), has similarly failed to produce any convincing data of destruction or repair traceable to the time of the Sasanian conquest and its aftermath.[47]

Both the Church of the Holy Zion on Mount Zion and the Church of the Holy Sepulchre are depicted in some of the literary sources as having been set ablaze by the Persian forces and to have subsequently undergone repair, being in addition the sites where, according to Strategios' account, a

---

40 Avni 2010.

41 Avi-Yonah 1949-50; Arubas – Goldfus 2005; on a destruction level at the Sheikh Bader complex that can be seen as attributable to the Persian conquest, cf. Schick 1995:340-341; Russell 2001:50. See now the negative verdict regarding such destruction layers at the Sheikh Bader complex in Avni 2010.

42 Barkay 1994; for the absence of a seventh-century destruction level at this complex, see Barkay 1994:89-90; Avni 2010.

43 Schick 1995:34, 332-333 (arguments that the church suffered some damage but continued to function throughout the period).

44 Ben-Dov 1982:240-241. Cf. Mare 1987:237 (who asserts that the church was destroyed by the Persian forces in 614).

45 Avni 2010; Russell defines the archaeological evidence for Persian destruction at the site of the *Nea Ekklesia* as "tenuous in the extreme" (Russell 2001:50).

46 Schick 1995:34, 333-334.

47 Russell 2001:50; Avni 2010.

considerable number of Jerusalem Christians were massacred by the invaders.[48] The archaeological data unearthed so far at the site of the Church of the Holy Zion, while as yet insufficient to allow a relatively complete reconstruction of its history in the late Byzantine and early Islamic periods, does not evince traces of destruction traceable to the early seventh century.[49] Significantly, the thorough archaeological exploration of the Church of the Holy Sepulchre has also been unable to reveal any traces of such early-seventh-century substantial damage and destruction or indeed indications of the extensive repairs alleged in the written sources.[50] The archaeological record at the Church of the Holy Zion and the Church of the Holy Sepulchre highlights thus the general difficulty of finding any secure evidence of the post-614 repair and restoration programme which the literary sources attribute either to the hegumen of the monastery of St. Theodosios, Modestos (who had assumed the duties of the exiled Patriarch Zacharias in his absence), or to the Sasanian Christian royal treasurer, Yazdīn.[51] This tends to demonstrate again that the damage possibly inflicted on ecclesiastical compounds such as the Church of the Holy Zion and the Church of the Holy Sepulchre was largely minor and the repair efforts were sufficiently minimal not to leave any discernible archaeological traces.[52] Furthermore, as with the residential compounds, a number of church and monastic complexes in and around Jerusalem show patterns of continuous use throughout the seventh century and into the early Islamic period, without any evident major

---

48 *Chronicon Paschale,* 704; *Khuzistan Chronicle,* 26-27; Strategios, *Expugnatio* 11.7 (Arabic version A), 23; Strategios, *La prise,* 11.7, 13.15, 23; Eutychius, *Annalen,* 119-120; for an overview of the sources referring to the repair of the Church of the Holy Sepulchre following its reported damage by fire during the Sasanian takeover of Jerusalem, see Schick 1995:37.

49 Cf. Schick 1995:335-336 (who states that the church has only "uncertain archaeological remains" but on the basis of the literary sources concludes that it was burned in 614, subsequently repaired and continued to function in the Byzantine-Umayyad transition period); cf. also Avni 2010, with conclusions that on the basis of the archaeological material published so far, it is still impossible to detect ash layers attributable to the Persian conquest but the church may have suffered minor damage which required some restoration effort.

50 Avni – Seligman 2003; Avni 2010; Avni – Seligman (forthcoming). On the controversial nature of the literary sources' claims for the damage inflicted on the Church of the Holy Sepulchre in 614, see also the earlier observations of Schick 1995:36-37; cf. Schick 2007:180.

51 Cf. Antiochus monachus, *Epistula*, 1427-1428; Strategios, *Expugnatio,* 24.e (Arabic version C); Eutychius, *Annalen*, 120; *Khuzistan Chronicle,* 26-27; Sebeos, 116-118.

52 See the observations in Avni 2010.

disruptions – hence the abandonment of monasteries and churches and the resultant detrimental effect on Christian life and worship, sometimes postulated on the basis of narrative sources, also cannot be supported by the archaeological record.[53]

At the same time, archaeological work at several mass burial sites in Jerusalem which were used in the Byzantine period indicated that one of them, the Mamila burial cave[54] can be dated to the early seventh century and its location generally corresponds to Strategius' description of the one of the sites where Christian victims of the Persian conquest of the city in 614 were entombed.[55] The data at the other sites is not unambiguous and can invite other interpretations and datings.[56] But at least in the case of the Mamila burial cave one encounters a rare broad agreement between a narrative source and the archaeological record as well as a confirmation that the Jerusalem Christian population did suffer heavy losses at the time of the Persian storming of the city in 614 (although the numbers of the deceased given in the literary sources are undoubtedly greatly exaggerated[57] and assigning a responsibility to what seems to be a massacre of Christians leading to the mass burial clearly retains an element of conjecture).[58]

On the whole, however, the archaeological evidence demonstrates that while during and in the immediate aftermath of the Persian conquest of Jerusalem the Christian population suffered the consequences of human losses and deportation to Persia, ultimately it did not have any long-standing effects on the urban and ecclesiastical infrastructure, and the continuity of settlement in the city and its hinterland was far less disruptive than the catastrophic picture elaborated in documentary sources.[59] The striking

---

53 See, for example, the more recent studies of Avner 2003; Amit – Seligman – Zilberbod 2003; Arubas – Goldfus 2005:16-17; Avner 2006-2007.

54 Reich 1994; Maeir 1994; Reich 1996; Maeir 2000:176-177; Naggar 2002. Cf. Also Breydy 1981.

55 Strategios, *Expugnatio,* 23.28; Strategios, *La prise,* 23.28.

56 Kloner 2003:137-138.

57 See also the summary of the evidence which can link some of the other Byzantine period burial sites in Jerusalem to the early seventh century in Avni 2010.

58 See the cautious observations of Cameron 2002:61-62.

59 See the overall conclusions on the short-term and long-term impact of the Sasanian conquest of Jerusalem on the Christian presence in the city and its environs in Avni 2010.

discrepancies between the archaeological and written record of the Sasanian capture of Jerusalem raises serious methodological questions regarding the manner in which the combined use of both kinds of evidence can be employed to reconstruct historical events or short-term and long-term political and religious developments.[60] All the more that similar disagreement between the archaeological data and textual sources also characterize the evidence of the Sasanian invasions of the Byzantine territories in Asia Minor, Syria and Egypt.[61]

In the case of the Sasanian conquest of Jerusalem some internal contradictions in the written sources, especially in the sermon of Strategios,[62] ultimately lend more credibility to the archaeological evidence, which indicates that whatever damage it may have inflicted on the city's ecclesiastical compounds, it was relatively minor as were the repair works reportedly ascribable either to Modestos or the Sasanian official Yazdīn. Similarly, a critical examination of the documentary and archaeological record of early seventh-century Sasanian rule in the occupied eastern Byzantine provinces reveals that far from being a violent and destructive break from Byzantine economic, social and cultural patterns, once Sasanian authority was established (and the resistance it encountered at places like Jerusalem overpowered with brutal force), it aimed to achieve stabilization and continuity with the preceding administrative system, maintaining also (on the whole) religious toleration and freedom.[63] The Sasanian occupying regime could interfere in the ecclesiastical politics in the conquered territories to further its own political interests, but also could be very cautious that its representative authorities did not give offense to the religious sensibilities of the local Christian population with their own Zoroastrian observances which reportedly appear to have been practiced rather discreetly.[64]

---

60 See the observations of Russell 2001:41-42, 51-52, 62-71; Avni 2010.

61 Foss 2003:164-165; Gariboldi 2009: *passim*.

62 On some internal contradictions in Strategios' sermon and on its incorporation of material which actually belies its anti-Persian tenor and claims, see now Howard-Johnson 2010:ch.6.

63 Foss 2003: *passim*; Mitchell 2007:413; Gariboldi 2009: *passim*.

64 See the hagiographic account of the characteristic encounters between the Sasanian authorities in Caesarea and St Anastasius of Persia, *Vita Anastasii,* cc. 16-30 (ed. Flusin:1, 56-75). See the observations of Fluisn:2, 232-243; Foss 2003:160-161; Howard-Johnson 2010:ch.6.

Thus apart from helping to reconstruct facets of the historical reality of the Sasanian invasion and occupation of Byzantine Palestine, the cautious use of archaeological research as a corrective to the written records of the Persian capture of Jerusalem in 614, with their dramatic and exaggerated accounts of Persian (and Jewish) anti-Christian violence and atrocities in Jerusalem and the wholesale destruction and conflagration of the city's Christian sacral architecture, including, most traumatically for Christendom, the Church of the Holy Sepulchre. This corrective also serves to bring into sharper focus the manner in which these narratives exploited anti-Persian and anti-Jewish stereotypes as well as the rhetorics of Christian typology which sought to set the contemporary Sasanian conquest of Jerusalem in the framework of paradigmatic biblical events, phraseology and allusions related to the earlier travails of the Holy City such as its devastation by the Babylonians in 586 BCE and the following Babylonian captivity.[65] It also further highlights the inescapable links between the propagandizing agenda underlying the graphic narratives of Persian anti-Christian cruelty and sacrilege in Strategios' sermon (which shows strong indications that it was a officially-commissioned work)[66] and the related notions of the religio-political complex used by Heraclius and his court to escalate the religious dimension of the warfare of the 620s. As this religio-political complex represents a radical (and in some respects singular) innovation in the theory and practice of the East Roman/Byzantine warfare, it is worth considering it in the general context of the formation and development of the Byzantine version of the just war tradition and the earlier East Roman - Sasanian Persian conflicts.

65 On the use of the rhetorics of Christian biblical typology in Strategios' sermon and Sophronios' Jerusalem anacreontic poems, see Wilken 1992:216-233; Olster 1998:79-84; Stemberger 1999:262-64.

66 Howard-Johnston 2004; Howard-Johnston 2010:ch.6.1, 163-171; ch.13.1, 420-423.

CHAPTER 2

CHRISTIAN IDEOLOGY OF WARFARE IN THE EAST ROMAN /BYZANTINE WORLD AND SASANIAN PERSIA

Late Antique and early medieval East Roman/Byzantine Eastern Orthodox attitudes to the problems of warfare, just and "holy" war offer important parallels to and differences from the respective contemporaneous Western Christian attitudes but have received much less scholarly attention than the corresponding attitudes to the same phenomena in Western Christianity. Lately an interesting debate has developed among Eastern Orthodox theologians and scholars centred on the historical development and transformations of the notions of "justifiable war" and "just war" or the categorization of war as a "lesser good" or "lesser evil" in Eastern Orthodox Christianity, from their scriptural and patristic foundations to more contemporary re-formulations.[67] However, it is still difficult to present a definitive reconstruction of the evolution of the notions of just and/or justifiable war in Eastern Orthodox religious and secular thought and societies, since some of the main relevant works in its classical representative tradition, Byzantine Christianity, have either not been edited and published, or when edited, have not been translated into modern Western European languages and thus remain inaccessible to the larger scholarly audience.[68] With the present state of evidence and research in this area of study, it is possible to chart what seem to be the most significant East Roman Christian/Byzantine Eastern Orthodox approaches to just and justifiable warfare in late antiquity and the early Middle Ages as well as their relevance to the intermittent conflicts with Sasanian Persia, while remaining conscious of the problems described above and the quantity of unpublished source material in this particular field.

As in late antique and early medieval Western Christianity, the roots of the prevailing attitudes to war and peace in East Roman Christian/Byzantine

67 One of the recent issues of *St Vladimir's Theological Quarterly* 47/1, 2003, has been entirely devoted to these debates. See also the relevant studies collected in Haldon 2007.

68 See, for example, the brief and cautious overview of this field in Miller 1995:11-12; cf. the observations of Haldon 1999:2-7, *passim*.

Orthodox thought can be easily traced back to the New Testament and its well-known passages concerning the use of force, violence, Christ's moral teaching and its emphatic pacifistic perspective (for example, Matthew 5–7, 26:52, Luke 2:14, 3:14, 6:29). At the same time, East Roman Christian/Byzantine Orthodox thought inherited the potential for a non-pacifistic and even militaristic exegesis of the New Testament passages containing military imagery (for example, 1 Thessalonians 5:8, Ephesians 6:10, 1 Corinthians 9:7, 2 Timothy 2:3–4), Jesus' "sword" allusions (Matthew 10:34, Luke 22:35–38) and the heavenly war imagery in Revelation 20, which, as in Western Christianity, in particular circumstances and through suitably literalist interpretations could be used to sanction the use of force and justify war efforts.

East Roman/Byzantine Christianity also inherited the evident tensions between the ideas of war and peace in the Old and New Testaments respectively, which, despite the continuity between notions of the ultimate universal eternal peace in some trends of Jewish prophetic and messianic thought and early Christian messianism, diverged substantially in other areas. These divergences had already caused divisions and schisms in early Christianity, as many of the Gnostic groups came to assign the Yahweh-inspired war and violence episodes in the Old Testament to an inferior (frequently seen as wicked) demiurge of the physical world. Marcion's (c.85–c.160) dichotomy between the New Testament God of salvation and love and the Old Testament God of the law of vengeance and justice also evolved into an influential trend in early Christianity until the early third century CE. Millenarian trends in early Christianity, Montanism, and other related apocalyptic currents, seeking to revive apostolic Christianity, characteristically professed fervent pacifism and a renunciation of violence. These pacifistic trends and tendencies in early Christianity could be accompanied both with apocalyptic expectations of a forthcoming eschatological peace and with the forceful rejection and denunciation of Christian participation in (Roman) military service. Versions of this anti-militarism and pacific views were shared and articulated with different degrees of intensity and emphasis by early Church Fathers such as St Justin Martyr (c.100–c.165), Clement of Alexandria (c.150–c.215), St Hippolytus (c.170–c.236), Tertullian (c.160–c.225), Origen (c.185–c.254), St Cyprian of Carthage (d.258), Arnobius (3rd–4th century) and Lactantius (c.250–

c.325).[69] At the same time, a growing amount of evidence suggests that Christians served in the Roman army in the pre-Constantinian era, especially from the late second century onwards, and were thus beginning to form Christian milieus within the Roman military apparatus.

Constantine the Great's Edict of Milan in 313, his conversion to Christianity and the legitimization and institutionalization of the Church in the Roman empire inevitably led to various patterns of rapprochement between the state's and the Church's approaches to war and its justification. This rapprochement is exemplified by Eusebius of Caesarea (c.260–c.340) but did occur against the background of the protests and opposition of anti-militarist Christian groups such as the Donatists. This newly evolving concord between lay and clerical authorities followed somewhat differing patterns in the West and East Roman empires, effected by the distinct ways in which Church–state relations developed in the Latin West (which amid the progress of the "barbarian" invasions and the establishment of the Germanic states were also able to trigger characteristic secular–ecclesiastic rivalries) and the Greek East (in the framework of the formation and crystallization of Byzantine political theology within a centralized imperial state).

In the Latin West where the very survival of the Christian empire, forced to wage defensive wars, was at stake, St Ambrose (c.339–397) and St Augustine (354–430) eventually laid the foundation of the medieval Western Christian just war tradition, which, through a process which has attracted extensive scholarly treatment, was systematized in the commentaries/syntheses of, for example, Gratian (d. by c.1160) and Thomas Aquinas (c.1225–1274). Adhering to a different corpus of patristic writings and a different set of relationships with the East Roman Christian/Byzantine state and ideology, the Eastern Orthodox Church retained important elements from pre-Constantinian Christian attitudes to war, its justification and ethics, which in East Roman Christian/Byzantine culture and thought co-existed with the inherited and maintained core elements of the secular just war tradition of the pre-Christian Roman empire and Greek antiquity. In the East

69 On the attitudes of the early Christian Fathers to participation in warfare and military service, see the principal patristic sources in Swift:1983. For studies of the problems raised by these attitudes, see Harnack 1905; Cadoux: 1919; Bainton 1946; Orselli: 1993; Field:1998.

Roman Christian world the pacific tendencies of pre-Constantinian Christianity were brought into the framework of the newly evolving Christian imperial ideology by figures such as Eusebius, St Cyril of Alexandria (376–444) and St John Chrysostom (345–407), who argued that the establishment of the Christian empire fulfilled a providential design to pacify the world and terminate humanity's violent conflicts and discord. Such notions drew to a certain degree on some earlier patristic views that even the pre-Constantinian *imperium romanum* had in reality provided favourable conditions for the spread and internationalization of Christianity, views that may betray some general indebtedness to earlier Stoic thinking about the pacifying role of the pre-Christian Roman empire.

However, not all of the Eastern Christian Fathers of the late East Roman/early Byzantine period were prepared unequivocally to identify the earthly Roman empire with the "empire of Christ". Coexistence between the pacific and pacifistic theological and social attitudes transmitted from early to Byzantine Christianity, on the one hand, and the political and military needs of an imperial state (which retained important features of pre-Christian Roman military structures, machinery and ethos), on the other, was understandably not always easy and unproblematic. A symptomatic manifestation of this tension is to be found in Eastern Orthodox Christian canon law - the well known 13th Canon of St. Basil the Great (c.330–379) from his first Canonical Epistle to Amphilochus, Bishop of Iconium (378), stipulates that the act of killing during war needs to be distinguished from voluntary murder, although it is advisable that the perpetrators should be refused communion for three years.[70] The text of the canon also contains an allusion to an earlier pronouncement by St. Athanasius of Alexandria (c.296–373) articulated in his Epistle to Ammoun the Monk, which (when extracted as a separate statement) states that it is "praiseworthy" to destroy adversaries in war.[71] When, however, the pronouncement is considered in the overall context of the rhetoric and imagery of the epistle, this can allow for different readings[72] which cast doubt on one of its possible interpretations as a rare and thus important Eastern Christian patristic endorsement of the lawfulness

70 *Syntagma*, vol. 4, 131. At the same time in his *Homily on Psalm 61.4* St. Basil stresses that a military vocation can be reconcilable with professing Christianity; on these and related pronouncements of St Basil, see also the observations of Swift, 1983:94-95.

71 *Syntagma*, vol. 4, 69.

72 See, for example, Harakas 1999:155–156; McGuckin 2006. Cf. Swift 1983:95.

of killing in war.[73] A succession of canons in the Apostolic Canons and those of the Ecumenical and Local Councils that entered Eastern Orthodox canon law lay down explicitly the prohibitions on Christian clergy and monks on entering military service or receiving positions in the secular state administration and government.[74] Stipulating further the prerogatives of clerical and monastic non-resistance to violence, these canonical regulations delineate the phenomenon that has been aptly defined as a "stratification of pacifism"[75] in the early medieval Church, applicable in varying degrees to the different Church activities in both the Greek East and the Latin West. Consequently, both clergy and monks were expected to maintain the high pacific and pacifistic standards of the early Church and were prohibited from any military activity, which was strictly reserved for the laity.

During the High Middle Ages the subsequent development of the inherited canon law of the patristic and early medieval periods followed differing trajectories in Western and Eastern Christendom. Between the eleventh and thirteenth centuries Catholic canonists, theologians and clerics introduced various innovations in Catholic canon law to accommodate and specify the role of the Church in the evolving Catholic just war and holy war doctrines (based generally on selective exegesis of the scriptural sources, the principal notions in Augustine's Christian justification of warfare and definitions of just war as well as Roman law) and the juridical theory of the Crusade. No comparable contemporary developments, however, can be detected in Eastern Orthodox Christian canon law[76] although since the First Crusade (1095-1099) Byzantine canonists were becoming increasingly acquainted with the war theology of the crusading movement, with its amalgamation of pilgrimage, just and holy war notions. Apart from these efforts to define and regulate the different aspects of Christian participation and responsibilities in warfare in the sphere of canon law, speculation on what should be the correct, adequate or acceptable Christian response to the reality of war and how to achieve the affirmation of peace remained

---

73 This line of interpretation is supported, for example, in Haldon 1999:26; Webster 2003:25-27.

74 See some of the texts of some of the relevant canons in Swift 1983:90-96.

75 See the discussion of this approach in Harakas 1981, 85ff.

76 On the attempts of the prominent twelfth-century Byzantine canonists John Zonaras and Theodore Balsamon to soften the harshness of the 13th Canon of St Basil and to consider it as an advisory rather than a mandatory canonical requirement, see Stoyanov 2009:170.

important areas in Eastern Orthodox theology, ethics and anthropology throughout the medieval period.

Indeed, while pacifistic and pacific currents in Eastern Orthodoxy may have maintained their currency in the medieval Byzantine world, the existing rapprochement between state and church in the late Roman and early Byzantine period meant that the Byzantine church frequently found itself in situations in which its support for and justification of Byzantine military campaigns was seen as highly significant and necessary. With or without imperial pressure, the Byzantine church could be involved in the mobilization of popular endorsement for Byzantine troops and inevitably was entrusted with ensuring that they observed their religious obligations properly and entered battle, to face danger and death, spiritually pure and in a pious frame of mind. As in Western Christendom, the involvement of Eastern Orthodoxy in the realm of medieval warfare found expressions in military religious services, the early entrance of military chaplains in the field army (who could also serve in the fleet), the celebration of Eucharistic liturgies in the field, the use of Christian religious symbolism and relics for military purposes, blessings of standards and weapons before battles, services for fallen soldiers after the cessation of fighting and thanksgiving rituals to celebrate victory.[77]

While focusing in great detail on the different aspects of warfare tactics and strategy, the various Byzantine military manuals such as the *Strategikon* attributed to Emperor Maurice (582-602) and the tract ascribed to Emperor Leo VI the Wise (886-912) also stipulate at some length the religious services that need to be performed in military camps and the religious duties of soldiers and priests.[78] Following on the paradigmatic use of the cross-shaped sign (the *labarum*) during Constantine the Great's victory over his rival Maxentius in the battle at the Milvian Bridge in 312, crosses either depicted on flags, or carried instead of or alongside standards, were widely used during Byzantine military campaigns. A number of reports recount the use of relics and well-known icons before and during battles between the

[77] On the military religious services in the Byzantine army, see Vieillefond:1935; McCormick 1986:238-251; Dennis 1993; on the late Roman period, see Bachrach 2003:13-19.

[78] *Strategikon* (ed. Mihăescu 1970; ed. Dennis – Gamillscheg 1981; transl. Dennis 1984); *Leonis Imperatoris tactica* (ed. Vári:1917-1922).

imperial troops and their adversaries. The wide-spread popularity and evolution of the cult of military saints such St. George, St. Demetrius of Thessalonike, St. Theodore Teron, St. Theodore Stratelates, etc., and their adoption as patrons by the Byzantine military aristocracy highlight another symptomatic dimension of the role of Eastern Orthodox religious culture in shaping the ethics and practice of warfare in the Byzantine Empire.[79]

The dialogue and debates between the secular and ecclesiastical authorities regarding the regulations, limits and various dimensions of Christian involvement in warfare continued throughout the history of the Byzantine empire. During the reign of warrior-Emperor Nikephoros II Phokas (963–969) the Constantinople Patriarch Polyeuktos (956–970) and the ecclesiastical hierarchy decided to invoke in a church synod the authority of St Basil's 13th Canon to deny the emperor's request that the Church should establish canonical regulations through which Byzantine soldiers who fell in warfare would begin to be honoured on a par with the holy martyrs and accordingly be celebrated with hymns and feast days.[80] Symptomatically, Nikephoros Phokas' request that fallen soldiers should be treated as martyrs occurred during the emperor's anti-Arab offensives in Asia Minor and Syria, re-conquests that witnessed a more pronounced use of religious rhetoric. It is also significant that the refusal of the Byzantine Church to treat fallen Christian soldiers as martyrs occurred after Pope Leo IV (847–855) and Pope John VIII (872–882) had already asserted that those who died defending the Church and Christendom would be granted absolution and receive heavenly rewards – notions that in the second half of the eleventh century would crucially contribute to the development and eventual formalization of the idea of crusading and the sanctification of holy war by the Catholic Church.

Within the Eastern Orthodox tradition comparable notions appear in the ninth-century *Vita Constantini* of the celebrated missionary to the Slavs, St. Constantine–Cyril the Philosopher (826/7–869), which records his ambassadorial visit to the court of the Abbasid caliph al-Mutawakkil (847–

---

79 On the rise and evolution of the cult of military saints in medieval Eastern Orthodox Christianity, see, for example, Delehaye:1909; Webster:1980.

80 Ioannis Skylitzes, *Synoposis* (ed. Thurn 1973:273–275).

861) in 851 and his debates with Muslim theologians there.[81] During these disputes he was asked by Muslim theologians why Christians do not apply in practice the precepts in the well-known verses in Matthew 5:38–44 teaching nonviolence, non-resistance to evil/evildoers and love and prayer for one's enemies. In his reported reply St Constantine in effect gave priority to the statement in John 15:13 ("No one has greater love than this, to lay down one's life for one's friends"), arguing that as private people Christians can bear any offenses, but when in company they defend each other and sacrifice their lives in battle for their neighbours. Accordingly, the martial feats of the "Christ-loving soldiers" in defense of their lands, the Holy Church and Christianity are interpreted through the prism of this precept in John as constituting paradigmatic Christian duties for which they should "fight to the last". After fulfilling these "precious pledges", the Church would qualify these Christian soldiers as martyrs and intercessors before God. But, unlike contemporary Catholicism, between the tenth and twelfth centuries this notion was not developed and affirmed systematically in Eastern Orthodoxy, and its rejection by Patriarch Polyeuktos during the aforementioned synod was an important precedent for its continuing negation by the Byzantine Church.

Byzantine theologians and canonists of the High Middle Ages were generally aware of the articulations and implications of the guarantees of martyrdom status and eternal heavenly life promised and elaborated in Western Christian crusading ideology to all those fighting in the name of Christ ever since Pope Urban II's seminal "holy war" sermon and appeal for a crusade at Clermont in 1095. Until the fall of Constantinople in 1453 on only two occasions did comparable but short-lived initiatives come from within the Byzantine Church, attempting, in the thirteenth and fourteenth centuries respectively, to promise remissions of sins and military martyrdom to Byzantine soldiers fighting in Anatolia.[82] Significantly, in the last century of the Byzantine period the prominent fourteenth-century Byzantine theologian and canonist Matthew Blastares confirms in his influential work on canon and civil law, *Syntagma kata stoicheon* (1355) the validity and relevance of the three-year penance of exclusion from communion

81 *Vita Constantini,* 6 (ed. Angelov – Kodov – Kuev) 1973:3, 93).

82 On these short-lived initiatives and their religio-historic context, see Stoyanov 2009:171-172.

prescribed in Basil's 13th Canon, rejecting earlier arguments against its harshness on the basis of his own scriptural and theological exegesis.[83]

Against the background of these enduring Byzantine attitudes to the Christian practice of warfare a symptomatic debate has developed lately among Byzantinists and medievalists in general focused on the religio-historical problem of whether Byzantium ever conceptualized and put into practice its own brand of wars fought for ostensibly religious purposes comparable to the contemporaneous jihad in Islam and the crusading warfare of Western Europe. This debate has brought to the attention of a wider scholarly audience some important but less well-known and often neglected evidence of the interrelations between Byzantine Orthodox Christianity, on the one hand, and Byzantine political and military ideology and warfare, on the other. The debate can be traced to the early stages of modern Byzantine studies – for instance, in the works of Gustave Schlumberger on tenth-century Byzantine history.[84] According to Schlumberger, the campaigns of Nikephoros Phokas and John I Tzimiskes (969–976) against the Arab Muslim powers in the Levant had a religious character and can be qualified as proto-crusades, especially as Tzimiskes aspired to re-conquer Jerusalem for Christendom. Schlumberger's views were followed by medievalists such as René Grousset[85] and George Ostrogorsky; the latter argued that Emperor Heraclius' daring counter-offensive against Sasanian Persia in 620s can be identified as the actual forerunner of the Western Crusades, and some of Tzimiskes' anti-Arab campaigns betray a "veritable crusading spirit".[86] At the other extreme, in his influential publication on the idea of holy war and the Byzantine tradition, Vitalien Laurent argued that, in contrast to the medieval Islamic and West European versions of holy war, for variety of reasons Byzantine Eastern Orthodoxy failed to develop a proper holy war tradition and thus, unlike Latin Europe, could not manage to find an active military response to medieval Islamic expansionism.[87]

---

83 *Syntagma*, vol. 4, 69.

84 Schlumberger 1890; Schlumberger 1896-1905.

85 Grousset 1934: 1, 15.

86 Ostrogorsky 1957:90, 263.

87 Laurent 1946:71-98.

The view that the notion of a "holy war", as developed in the Islamic and West European holy war ideologies, remained alien and inconceivable to medieval Byzantine culture has since been upheld and supported with more arguments and evidence by a number of distinguished historians and theologians. With varying degrees of certainty and emphasis they have endorsed different aspects of the thesis that Byzantium did not develop a holy war tradition and abhorred (or in the case of the crusading movement, also did not comprehend) the holy war doctrines that arose and matured in the medieval Islamic Near East and Western Europe. In many cases, the absence of a real crusade ideology (in West European terms) in medieval Byzantium is attributed to the specific nature of Byzantine Orthodoxy, its institutions and approach to violence and warfare.[88] The proponents of this thesis habitually approach Byzantine military history (and its religio-political ramifications) in the context of contemporaneous Islamic and West European theories and practice of holy war and their shared features. These features include: the proclamation (and leadership) of the holy war by a "legitimate" religious authority (warfare is thus seen as decreed by God); the ostensible religious aims of the war, which needs to be seen as being waged against adversaries identified in a religious context as "infidel" or "heretic" – these aims can be thus in theory virtually unlimited; and the promise of spiritual rewards to the warriors (remission of sins, martyrdom, eternal salvation, entrance into paradise). In this line of argument, since Byzantine military history only sporadically shows elements of these features (and as a rule only in embryonic from), the inevitable conclusion is that Byzantium did not develop and put into practice an ideology of a Christian holy war.

Historians who argue that the study of the Byzantine version of Christian warfare needs to take into account to a much greater degree East Roman/Byzantine political and religious developments on their own terms reach somewhat different conclusions,[89] although their arguments may differ in accent and approach. In their line of argument, some of the criteria used to define holy war ideology in Islamic and West European contexts are not applicable to Eastern Christendom and Byzantium. Thus, the fact that it was the Byzantine emperor who declared and conducted the various Byzantine

---

88 See, for example, Lemerle:1955, 617ff.; Oikonomidès 1995; Dennis 2001; Dagron 1997; Laiou 1993; Laiou 2006.

89 Kolia-Dermitzakē 1991; Kolbaba 1998. See also the re-assessments of this thesis in Haldon 1999:13-34; Stephenson 2007; Carile 2005: *passim*.

wars and military expeditions should not automatically lead to the conclusion that these wars were entirely secular, because Byzantine political and religious ideology could not be separated so easily. In Byzantine political theology, the emperor was extolled as Christ's vicar and God's chosen ruler to preside over and defend the God-elected Christian Roman empire, itself an earthly replica of the divine heavenly monarchy. As a defender of the True Faith, Orthodoxy, his God-granted mission was to lead his armies against those who threatened the integrity of the universal Christian empire and its providential mission – whose enemies thus were also enemies of Orthodoxy. Regaining lost imperial lands, therefore, also meant restoring and expanding Orthodox Christianity, a notion that could be used to justify offensive warfare. In reality, Byzantine wars were always seen as being waged in defense of the unity of the sole legitimate Christian empire and Orthodoxy, which attached a certain quality of "holiness" to these war efforts, regarded consequently as divinely ordained and supported.

The debate on the existence or non-existence of a Byzantine version of Christian holy war has undoubtedly opened new important venues for the exploration of Eastern Orthodox perspectives on the ethics and theology of warfare from the late Roman and early Byzantine to the late Byzantine period. In some of the spheres of this debate and with the present state of published evidence and research, definitive conclusions cannot be reached as yet. Debating Byzantine military history in greater depth, however, has brought about a deeper understanding of some of the specifically Eastern Christian and Byzantine approaches to the ethics and conduct of warfare. In an important contrast with the medieval West, for example, in Eastern Christendom and Byzantium, ecclesiastical involvement and participation in warfare with some religious goals was important but not absolutely vital for its promulgation and legitimization. The various Byzantine treatises on military strategy and tactics for combat[90], moreover, shed further light on the distinct Byzantine attitudes towards the interrelationship of Christianity and warfare and its ethical implications. These tracts often draw heavily on earlier Hellenistic and Roman authorities, which highlights the continuity of the tradition of tactical and strategic manuals from Graeco-Roman antiquity to the Byzantine Middle Ages, but they inevitably contain much material and

90 See the three Byzantine military treatises in Denis (ed. and transl. 1981); *Strategikon* (ed. Mihăescu 1970; ed. Dennis – Gamillscheg 1981); (transl. Dennis 1984); *Leonis Imperatoris tactica* (ed. Vári:1917-1922).

advice reflecting Byzantine Christian stances on warfare. They emphasize one of the undisputed features of the Byzantine version of Christian just war which represented a characteristic East Roman/Byzantine synthesis between the inherited Roman political military ideology, existing Christian religio-political pacific models and rhetoric and post-Constantinian political theology.

Despite the ongoing general expansion of the study of the various facets of East Roman/Byzantine-Sasanian Persian relations in late antiquity, with a major focus on their military conflicts, the application and adaptation of the East Roman/Byzantine tradition of just war (which was simultaneously undergoing its Christianization) to these relations and conflicts has received much less attention. Characteristically, while discussing Persian methods and tactics of warfare the well known Byzantine military treatises such the *Strategikon* attributed to Maurice and *Περὶ Στρατηγικῆς* (*De Re Strategica*), do not introduce any religious dimension to the subject matter; the former reiterates in its Persian section some general anti-Persian stereotypes, whereas the latter alludes to several past episodes of military history involving confrontations with Persian forces.[91]

Against the background of sporadically erupting Romano-Iranian hostilities and periods of a quest for a *modus vivendi* between the two empires, in a time of conflict their respective propaganda machines could portray their military operations as a just war response to offensive warfare started by the respective imperial adversary, thus aiming also for the higher moral ground.[92] The competing but differing assertions of East Roman and Sasanian imperial universalisms (in their religio-political essence and manifestations) also played their role in the respective conceptualizations and justifications of this inter-imperial warfare by the two sides, as did the inherited Roman fears of and claims for the existence of an aggressive Achaemenid-oriented Sasanian irredentism (Herodian, *History*, 6, 2.2;

---

91 *Strategikon* 11.1 (ed. Mihăescu 1970:262-268); *Περὶ Στρατηγικῆς* 19.75, 33.15, 41.14, 43.25 (ed. Dennis 1981:66, 102, 120, 126). On the Persian military vocabulary in the *Strategikon*, see Freshfield 1947:4-5, 23-24, 31. Generally, on the classical inheritance in *Περὶ Στρατηγικῆς* and the *Strategikon*, see now Luttwak 2009:258ff., 266-304.

92 See, for example, the episodes highlighting the use of just war, and *ius in bello* norms-related propaganda in Roman-Persian relations in Rubin 1998; Fowden 1993:25-28; Frendo 1997:107-108.

Ammianus Marcellinus, *Res Gestae*, 17, 5.1-8) aiming to effect a reconquest of the Roman territories which were formerly part of the Achaemenid realm.[93] Existing and newly evolving Roman stereotypes regarding Persia and the Persians could also be used in East Roman war-related propaganda and accounts of Roman-Sasanian hostilities[94] alongside the standard notion of Roman invincibility.[95] As evidenced by Procopius' heightened emphasis on and attribution of religious aspects to Sasanian-East Roman conflicts in the sixth century, the religious dimension of the long-standing inter-imperial rivalry was receiving a growing attention and articulation in the East Roman world during the reign of Justinian.[96]

The existence, status, ecclesiastical affiliation and loyalties of the Christian communities of Sasanian Persia represented a special factor which deepened the religious dimension of Roman-Sasanian political rivalry and made the fortunes of these communities dependent on the vicissitudes of this inter-imperial struggle,[97] as guarantees for their religious freedoms eventually came to be negotiated and regulated in diplomatic agreements and peace treaties between the two empires. The Sasanian treatment of these Christian communities could be conditioned by political and strategic considerations vis-à-vis the Roman empire even before the Constantine initiated his first pro-Christian policies in 313. The subsequent progress of

93 On the ongoing debate whether the Sasanian dynasty considered itself a successor to the Achaemenids and professed territorial irredentist ambitions about the former Achaemenid territories which formed part of the late antique *imperium romanum*, cf., for example, Yarshater 1971; Whitby:1988:212-213; Gnoli 1989:122, 136 ff.; Rubin 1998; Shahbazi 2001 Shahîd 2004:226-227, 238-244.

94 On the use of such Sasanian-related stereotypes in Roman propaganda (literary and visual) and historiographical contexts before Heraclius' reign, see, for example, Suolahti 1947; Cameron 1969, *passim*; Pugliese Carratelli 1971; Frendo 1997 *passim*; Teitler 1999; Smith 1999; Drijvers 2006:48-57; Schneider 2006:242-247. On stereotypes and notions regarding Rome in Sasanian imperial propaganda, see, for example, Rubin 1998; Wiesehöfer 2005a.

95 On the exploitation of the notion of Roman invincibility in a Christianized context of a conflict with Sasanian Persia, see Frendo 1997:106-107, 115.

96 See the analysis of Procopius' narratives superimposing religious features on and interpretations of East Roman-Sasanian Persian antagonisms in Frendo 1997:107-115 *passim*.

97 For an early study of Christianity in Sasanian Persia, exemplifying some of the earlier approaches to the problem, see Labourt 1904; for a recent and up-to-date study, see Panaino 2004 (with extensive bibliographies).

Christianization of *imperium romanum* in the fourth century (accompanied by new Roman-Persian conflicts) lead to the politicization of their perceived status and role in Sasanian society, suspicions of disloyalty and outbreaks of anti-Christian persecution.[98]

Symptomatically, in his *Vita Constantini* 4.13 Eusebius reproduces a letter which, he asserts, Constantine dispatched c. 324/325 to the Sasanian monarch Šābuhr II (309-379) regarding the situation of the growing Christian communities in Persia. In this letter (whose historicity is under debate) Constantine appeals to the Šāhān Šāh to protect and treat humanely his numerous Christian subjects, thus positioning himself as a self-declared protector and benefactor of the Christians in the Sasanian realm.[99] In 337, the last year of Constantine's reign, Roman-Persian tensions, especially in religiously contested Transcaucasia (in this case, over the religious affiliations of Armenia), were escalating again, and evidence of the emperor's war preparations (amid which he died, hence hostilities began under his Constantius II in 338) suggests that he was planning an anti-Sasanian campaign with some discernible religious aspects.[100] As demonstrated by the contemporaneous *Demonstration* 5, "On Wars", of Aphrahat, the first of the Syriac Church Fathers, at least some Christians in the Sasanian realm were contemplating and hoping for a Christian Roman victory over Sasanian Persia in the Near East, anticipations accompanied with eschatological expectations.[101]

---

98 On this religio-political context of the development of Christianity in fourth-century Sasanian Persia, see, for example, Decret 1979; Chaumont 1988.

99 For a recent survey of the debate on the authenticity of Constantine's letter to Šābuhr in Eusebius' *Vita Constantini* 4.13 and its implications, see Frendo 2001.

100 See the observations of Decret 1979:139; Brock 1982a:7; Barnes 1981:257; Barnes 1985:132-133 (Barnes defines Constantine's planned campaign against Šābuhr as a "religious crusade" intended to establish a Christian Roman on the Sasanian throne); Fowden 1993:94-97 (arguments that Constantine's planned anti-Persian war was intended to launch a "crusade for world empire", both Christian and Roman, marking the beginning of God's kingdom, as already announced in 335 by Eusebius in *De Laudibus Constantini* 16.6); Whitby 2002a:71 (recognition of "crusading overtones" of Constantine's pre-war "propaganda about the liberation of Christians in Mesopotamia"); cf. the more cautious approach in Frendo 2001:63ff.; for a discussion of the contemporaneous evidence of Constantine's planned anti-Sasanian campaign, see Fowden 1994:146-153.

101 Aphrahat, *Demonstration* 5 (ed. Pereira 1906); discussion in Brock 1982a:7-8; Barnes 1985:133-135; Fowden 1993:96

The changed geopolitical situation in the early fifth century provided much more favourable conditions not only for the continuation but for the growth of Christianity in Sasanian Persia, at least until the last years of Yazdagird I's reign (399-420), and the Christian communities succeeded in re-organizing and stabilizing their church organization. Significantly, in 424 the Christian church of Sasanian Persia achieved independence from the Patriarchate of Antioch, making it possible for its prelates to minimize its formal links with the ecclesiastical establishment of the Eastern Roman Empire in the eyes of the Sasanian authorities. The Christological controversies and divisions of the fifth century led to the estrangement of the Christian church of Sasanian Persia (now headed by its own *katholikós* residing in Seleucia-Ctesiphon) from the patriarchates of Rome, Constantinople, Alexandria and Antioch (and from 451, Jerusalem). In 431 the Third Oecumenical Council held in Ephesus deposed the Constantinople Patriarch Nestorius (428-431) and denounced his Christological teachings of the two separate Persons in the Incarnate Christ, respectively Divine and Human. The Fourth Oecumenical Council in 451, which took place in Chalcedon, re-asserted the Christological formula of "One Person in Two Natures" in the "Definition of Chalcedon" but it was rejected by a number of Eastern Christian theologians and communities which came to adhere to versions of the Christological position that Christ possesses one nature (hence they are generally categorized by the umbrella term "Monophysite"). Factors such as the influx of Nestorian Christians into Sasanian Persia contributed to the Nestorianization of its church by the end of the fifth century which further emphasized its division from the Chalcedonian church of the Eastern Roman empire. In the sixth century the Monophysite Christian communities also increased in numbers and influence in Sasanian Persia, strengthened also by Monophysite refugees compelled to settle on Persian territory by anti-Monophysite measures in the eastern Roman provinces.

From its establishment as an autonomous body until the end of the Sasanian empire, the ecclesiastical elite of the Christian church of Sasanian Persia was bound to strive to foster and maintain good and close links with the Šāhān Šāh: on occasion the *katholikós* would join the Šāhān Šāh and his entourage on his military campaigns and members of the church hierarchy could be used as Sasanian ambassadors.[102] These associations needed to be

[102] See Garsoïan 1973; Sako 1986.

maintained vis-à-vis the religious and political priorities of the Zoroastrian clergy which was notably apprehensive of the proselytising potential and successes of the church, especially in the case of conversions to Christianity among Sasanian noble and priestly families. The fortunes of the Christian denominations in Sasanian Persia could thus be affected by the shifting balance of power between the Sasanian monarchy and the Zoroastrian priestly establishment (with its pronounced, at times, anti-Christian stance) as well as by the tensions and frictions between the Nestorian, Monophysite and Chalcedonian (much smaller in number and influence) Christian communities in the empire.

At the same time, the Sasanian monarchy was prepared to acknowledge (in the framework of its diplomatic relations and formal treaties with the Eastern Roman Empire in 422 and 561-562) the role of the Christian Roman emperor as a champion and guardian of the Christians in Persia. Both agreements contained provisions guaranteeing their freedom to practice their religion without obstruction[103] – a prerogative sought by Constantine in the 320s. As in the fourth century, however, such inter-imperial religio-political inter-dependencies could make the status of Christian denominations in Sasanian Persia vulnerable in wartime periods when their loyalty to the Iranian monarchy could be judged in accordance with the extent of their perceived religious affiliation with the Roman imperial adversary. Conversely, Jewish communities in the Sasanian Persia found themselves far less frequently the target of suspicion and suppression for reasons which included the lack of such dangerous religio-political connotations that could be exploited to question their loyalty to the Sasanian crown. Indeed the nature of the religious and political loyalties of the Christian communities of Sasanian Persia and their self-identification pose one of the most difficult and intriguing problems related to the religious history of the empire.[104]

This formalized recognition by the Sasanians of the Eastern Roman empire as a protector of the Christians of Persia seemed important enough in the framework of the agendas and ambitions of the imperial Chalcedonian

---

[103] On these treaties and their provisions, envisaging and guaranteeing religious freedoms for the Christians of Sasanian Persia and their implications, see, for example, Verosta 1965; Guillaumont 1969-70; Schippmann 1990:42; Schmidt 2002:131ff.; Winter-Dignas 2007:137, 138-148, 226-227.

[104] Cf. Brock 1982a; Panaino 2010.

church to bring the Iranian-based Nestorian and Monophysite communities into the Chalecedonian fold. But it also provided in theory the possibility of a religiously-motivated *casus belli* through which infringements of the religious rights and freedoms of the Christians in Sasanian Persia could be used by its Eastern Roman imperial rival as a pretext for triggering a military conflict with a religious dimension. Significantly, the Eastern Roman war against Sasanian Persia in 421-422 (which lead to the peace treaty of 422, envisaging that both parties should respectively ensure toleration for Zoroastrians in Christian imperial territories and Christians in Persia) was launched to a great extent as a response to Sasanian anti-Christian persecution c. 420 during which Christian refugees fled to Roman territory.[105] The Constantinople imperial government sought to imbue the war effort with some religious import and the ideology of Christian triumphalism, acting as a benefactor to the Jerusalem see while endeavouring to make full use of the victory symbolism of the Golgotha Cross at the Holy Sepulchre in the ideological build up to the conflict.[106] According to the account of the war in Theodoret of Cyrrhus' (c. 393 – c. 457) *Ecclesiastical History* 5.36, the Persian armies received providential punishment for their militarist bellicosity by invading imperial territory, as did the blasphemy and threats against the Christian faith of a Persian commander during the Persian siege of Theodosiopolis (Erzerum). First, the dangerous Persian invasion is halted by a providentially sent storm and then the besieging Persian commander, threatening to burn Theodosiopolis' 'temple of God', is killed by a ballista, commanded 'in the name of the Lord' and 'christened' after the Apostle Thomas by Bishop Eunomius (in charge of the defense of the city), a providential chastisement which prompts the Persian forces to abandon the siege.

Like the accounts of Constantine's preparation for war against Sasanian Persia in 337, Theodoret of Cyrrhus' narrative of the conflict in 421-422 characteristically introduces Christian notions and practices in late antique warfare against the Sasanian imperial rival and recurrent adversary. One of the intentions of such religiously-coloured narratives and practices was to boost the morale and motivation of the Christian Roman troops, bringing a manifest religious dimension (much less pronounced in the pre-Christian

[105] On the background and course of the war, see the sources assembled in Greatrex – Lieu 2002:36-42.

[106] On the religious elements in the preparation and justification of the war, see Holum 1977.

Roman period) to this aspect of the preparation and conduct of warfare.[107] Stories of Christian miracles and miraculous visions forcing Persian armies to discontinue sieges of Roman cities also came in circulation as in the case of Šābuhr II' third siege of Nisibus in 350[108] and Xusraw Anusrovan's attempt to capture Sergiopolis (protected by the relics of the "victorious martyr, St. Sergius) in 542.[109] The protective military role of holy relics and images was also highlighted in popular narratives such as the story of the miracles of the Image of Edessa, the Holy Mandylion, which compelled the Sasanian Šāhān Šāh Xusraw I Anōšag-ruwān (531-579) to halt his assaults on Edessa in 544 and retreat, admitting that he could not prevail over the Christian God.[110] The salvationist power attributed to holy relics could be sought to raise the spirits of Eastern Roman Christians facing Persian military onslaughts, as in the case of the display of fragments of the "saving and life-giving" True Cross in Apamaea in 540 when it was under threat of being overrun by the armies of Xusraw I. The role of Bishop Eunomius in masterminding the defense of Theodosiopolis against the besieging Persian forces illustrates the military functions that the bishops of Eastern Roman cities under Persian attack frequently assumed (including acting as negotiators in times of conflict or overseeing the building of fortifications in areas which might be endangered by Persian invasion)[111] in a process of the militarization of episcopal duties which represents another religious aspect of the warfare between the Eastern Roman empire and Sasanian Persia in late antiquity.

Thus by the time Xusraw II chose to interfere in internal Byzantine political struggles to initiate the last great war of antiquity, the evolving Christian Eastern Roman ideology of warfare had left a discernible imprint on various areas of the interrelations between the two empires, ranging from the diplomatic interchange to military confrontations, coloured also by the issue of the Christians under Sasanian suzerainty. Given the intermittent nature of the East Roman-Persian wars of late antiquity, it is not surprising that Sasanian Persia would frequently figure as a brutal adversary in

[107] On this change of attitude (brought by the Christianization of the Roman empire) towards the role of religion in fostering and upholding military morale, see Whitby 1998:192-194.

[108] *Chronicon Paschale*, 536-539.

[109] Evagrius Scholasticus, *Ecclesiastical History*, 4.28.

[110] Evagrius Scholasticus, *Ecclesiastical History*, 4.27.

[111] On these military function of bishops during Eastern Roman-Sasanian Persian hostilities, see Whitby 1998:199-200.

Christian accounts of military conflicts involving divine intervention. At the same time, Persia enjoyed a special status in the East Roman *Weltanschauung*, both conceptually and on the politico-military plane, as a "legitimate" entity which was to be distinguished from the "barbarian" and "uncivilized" other powers of the non Graeco-Roman world.[112] This specific and ambiguous status of the Sasanian imperial state in East Roman perceptions could be exploited in Persia-related propaganda rhetoric and historiographic narratives (especially in times of conflict or pre-conflict preparation) to invest Sasanian-Roman collisions with a heightened religious significance, a trend which intensified during Justinian's reign.[113] Characteristically, the speech by which, according to Theophylact Simocatta, the Roman army commander Justinian tried to lift the spirit of his troops before an engagement with the Persian armies of Xusraw I in 576 uses some just war rhetoric but also contrasts Christianity with the Persian belligerent and "false religion" and its "unjust altars".[114] The speech also aims to convince the Roman soldiers that they are recruited by angels who would be recording the names of the fallen ones and awarding them with a higher, heavenly recompense,[115] but given the time of writing of Theophylact's *History* it may have projected back notions developed in the religiously charged wartime rhetoric of Heraclius' anti-Persian campaigns of the 620s.[116] Portraying the Sasanian Persian regime and its dynasty in times of hostilities as religious enemies (or adversaries of Christianity in general) could also bring strategic dividends in the sphere of the Sasanian-East Roman rivalry over the loyalties of the non-Chalcedonian Christian communities under Persian suzerainty.

Contemporaneous representations of Heraclius' counter-offensive predictably re-iterate the precepts of the late antique East Roman just war tradition, dwelling on the reconquest of the invaded and occupied imperial territories, and, in the new circumstances, the defense of the imperial capital

112 See, for example, the discussion of this specific status of Sasanian Persia in Ammianus Marcellinus' Persian-related narratives and characterizations in Drijvers 2006:65-66; on the civilizational "legitimacy" of Sasanian Persia in East Roman/Byzantine *Weltanschauung* (even in times of conflict), see, for example, Carile 1994:63-64; Carile 2000:191-192.

113 On this trend during Justinian's reign, see Frendo 1997:107-115.

114 Theophylact Simocatta, *History*, 3.13, esp. 3.13.13-16.

115 Theophylact Simocatta, *History*, 3.13.20.

116 As suggested in Whitby 1998:194.

Constantinople. But it is their portrayal of Heraclius' campaigns as being fought on behalf of Christians and Christian causes that has attracted attention and dispute, as their religious significance was amplified to a degree so far unprecedented in the history of East Roman-Sasanian Persian warfare. The striking evocation of Christian sentiment and militarist rhetoric during these campaigns have been on a number of occasions seen as sufficient to characterize them as a kind of a "proto-crusade" or "crusade" – or at least comparable in important respects to the crusading ideology of warfare.[117] Such interpretations make Heraclius' Persian wars central not only to the debate on whether Byzantium forged its own version of the Christian holy war tradition[118] but also to the study of the formation and evolution of holy or religious war theory and practice in medieval Christendom as a whole. While the latter more general problematic remains outside the scope of this monograph, the next chapter intends to contribute to the debate on the place of religious war notions in Heraclius' anti-Sasanian and the post-Heraclian Byzantine ideology of warfare by an analysis and re-assessment of the areas in which Heraclius' religiofication, justification and conduct of the war differed from earlier Eastern Roman-Sasanian Persian conflicts with discernible religious aspects. It also intends to offer a reconsideration of the impact that the fall of Jerusalem and the Holy Land to Xusraw's forces in 614 had on the rhetoric of the Byzantine reconquest of the 620s with its characteristic eschatological overtones.

---

[117] For approaches to Heraclius' Persian wars which employ some kind of a "crusade" terminology, whether used as a metaphor or a legitimate term, to define their religio-military essence, see, for example, Ostrogorsky 1957:90, 263; Vasiliev 1952:197; Shahîd 1972:302, 313; Impellizzeri 1985; Fowden 1993:35, 98; Whitby 2002a:60, 71; Mitchell 2007:418. On the adequacy of the use of such "crusade" terminology to characterize these early seventh-century wars, see, for example, the reservations of Lemerle 1955; Frendo 1997:105; Tyerman 2006:35; Farrokh 2007:262 (although that Farrokh also argues that Heraclius was "able to frame the war in terms of a Christian religious crusade", 256).

[118] See, for example, Kolia-Dermitzakē 1991:ch.5; Howard-Johnston 1994:84-85; Kolbaba 1998:203, 208; Howard-Johnston 1999 39-40; Whitby 1998:195; Dennis 2001:34-35; Laiou 2006:33.

CHAPTER 3

XUSRAW II'S WARTIME PERSIA (603-628): THE RELIGIOUS AND APOCALYPTIC ENEMY

The conceptualization of the Christian East Roman/Byzantine warfare may have been in essence a continuation of the largely secular late Roman just war tradition (understood as intended to defend imperial territories, regain lost territories and protect imperial subjects), but this tradition inevitably had been subjected to a process of Christianization which began as early as the reign of Constantine. In the maturing Christianized version of this Roman ideology of warfare it was the divinely ordained mission of the Christian Romans (the new "chosen people") to safeguard Constantinople, seen as both the "New Rome" and the "New Jerusalem", and its single universal Christian empire, the "New Israel", against the encroachments of the new "barbarians": first pagans, in later periods Muslims and, on occasion, West European Christians. This Christianized "just war" tradition became a fundamental part of Byzantine imperial ideology, closely interwoven with the reinterpreted and actualized Romano-Byzantine paradigms of God-guidedness in battle and imperial victory ("Victoria Augustorum").

Furthermore, Christian East Roman/Byzantine medieval military religious ideology shared with its Western and other Eastern Christian counterparts a dependence upon and exploitation of the Old Testament narratives and pronouncements of the God-commanded and-ordained wars of the Israelites against the "heathen" and "idolatrous" Canaanites. As representatives of the new "Chosen People", Byzantine emperors, ideologues and propagandists (and their Western Christian counterparts) could draw on these models to depict their wars as God-guided campaigns against the new "infidel" or "God-fighting" enemies. Accordingly, successful warrior-emperors and commanders could be compared to the kings of Israel or to paradigmatic figures in the Old Testament Israelite "holy" wars such as Moses, Aaron, Joshua and David. Thus, in Byzantine military religious ideology and art, Moses' crossing of the Red Sea could be interpreted as prefiguring Constantine the Great's victory at Milvian Bridge, and Joshua's military exploits and triumphs could be presented as alluding to

Nikephoros Phokas' and John Tzimiskes' victories on the battlefield. The enemies of Byzantium could be "recognized" as new versions of the Old Testament adversaries and oppressors of the Israelites such as the Assyrian king Sennacherib, acting again as instruments of God's punishment, provoked by the Byzantine sins.

The Sasanian invasion and occupation of the eastern Byzantine provinces in the first two stages of the war needed to be conceptualized in similar frameworks, but the Persian conquest of the Holy Land and Jerusalem made the religious stakes extremely high, as did the reports of Jewish military alliance with the Persian invaders,[119] anti-Christian atrocities and wholesale destruction of Christendom's most precious sites in the Holy City. In order to fully grasp the manner in which Xusraw II's capture of Byzantine Palestine and Jerusalem changed the complexion of Byzantine-Sasanian warfare after 614 and the far-reaching implications of the reported Sasanian-Jewish alliance during the invasion (leading to a short-lived (but disturbing to Christian sensitivities) Jewish ascendancy in Jerusalem, one needs to briefly chart first the evolving Christian East Roman perspectives on the Holy Land and the Holy City, from the inauguration of their Christianization under Constantine to their Sasanian occupation, which were closely intertwined with the changed attitudes to Jews and Judaism in the Christian Pax Romana.

The end and aftermath of the Byzantine-Sasanian war in 628 and the recovery of Jerusalem and Palestine was also marked by a hardening of official Byzantine (secular and ecclesiastical) attitudes to Jews and Judaism, resulting in anti-Jewish measures and crackdowns (especially in the Holy Land). This hardening was already evident in the reactions to the reported Sasanian-Jewish collaboration during the conquest of Palestine and Jerusalem which to a great extent were rooted in the important changes in the secular, religious and legal attitudes towards Jews from the late Roman into the early Byzantine period. The continuity and innovations in the inherited legal status of Byzantine Jews and Judaism, for example, as a *religio licita* (a "permitted religion" with its associated civil and political rights) in imperial legislation highlight the changing religious climate in the empire inevitably transformed by the advancing process of its Christianization in the wake of Constantine's Edict of Milan in 313.

---

[119] See note 123 below.

These legislative innovations and amendments often reflect the new stages of Jewish-Christian interrelations during the process of Christianization of *imperium romanum* when the earlier patterns of Jewish-Christian co-existence, controversies and rivalries were undergoing substantial revisions and readjustments. Such legal rulings affected both the Jewish communities in late Roman Palestine and those in the Greek-speaking diaspora of the empire. The new Christian Roman imperial enactments and measures implemented during the reigns of Constantius II (337-361), Arcadius (395-408), Theodosius I (379-395), prescribed various prohibitions and restrictions for Jews in the political, military, legal and social spheres, while maintaining the status of Judaism as a legally permitted cult and largely refraining from harsh economic discrimination. The socio-religious autonomy of Jewish communities within the imperial state was thus retained despite the effective disestablishment of the office of the *Nasi*, the so-called "Patriarch of the Jews" in the Holy Land in 429. The newly introduced Jewish-related legislation was codified (along with some novel restrictions) during the rule of Theodosius II's (408-450) in the *Codex Theodosianus*, with its far-reaching impact on medieval Christendom's legal treatment of the Jews.

During this period of crystallization of the new legal situation of the Jews, on occasion Jewish communities sought imperial intervention and protection in times of inter-communal Jewish-Christian conflicts or anti-Jewish violence. At other times imperial intervention checked Jewish groups involved in urban riots or (reportedly) in anti-Christian violence and imperial forces ruthlessly suppressed Jewish (and Samaritan) revolts and riots. The Jewish communities in Palestine were further affected by the sustained Christian Roman endeavours, initiated originally by Constantine the Great and his mother, St Helena (c.255–c.330), to Christianize Palestine by promoting devotional pilgrimage, appropriating Jewish biblical sites and actively erecting churches and monasteries at Christian holy places. The Christian "re-discovery" and infatuation with the physical Holy Land and Jerusalem led to the flourishing of Palestinian monasticism in the fifth century and the elevation of the Jerusalem see to a Patriarchate in 451.[120] As religious and ecclesiastical agendas increasingly came to dominate imperial

---

[120] On the Christianization of the Holy Land in the post-Constantinian era, cf. for example, Wilkinson 1977; Linder 1979; Hunt 1982; Groh 1985; Walker 1990; Hirschfeld 1992; Wilken 1992; Taylor 1993:86-342; Prawer 1996:317-331;Tsafrir 1999; Jacobs 2004:139-175.

policy towards the Jews, the Christianization process in the Holy Land was underlain by the church's supersessionist theology recognizing itself as the "True Israel" or the "New Israel", triumphant over the rejected "Old Israel", which, zealously maintained in patristic and ecclesiastical anti-Jewish polemics of the period,[121] further prompted campaigns of de-Judaization of biblical holy sites and the "Holy City" of Jerusalem.

Along with political factors, a continuing awareness of the ancient Jewish dimension of post-Constantinian Jerusalem, as evidenced by the still surviving Second Temple monuments and abandoned ruins on the desacralized Temple Mount, contributed to recurrent re-enactments of Hadrian's decree after the Bar Kokhba revolt of 132-135 CE prohibiting Jewish residence in the city and its environs. The strength of Christian sensibilities about the undying Jewish expectations of Jewish return to Jerusalem and the rebuilding of the Temple can be ascertained in the vehement Christian reactions against Julian's (361-363) short-lived attempts to re-build the Temple in the wake of his public overtures to Judaism in late 362.[122]

In late Roman and early Byzantine rulings legal attitudes and treatment of the Jews evidently compared favourably with that of the increasingly heavily criminalized Christian heretic. The reign of Justinian I ((527-565), however,

---

[121] On patristic and ecclesiastical attitudes to Jews and Judaism and Christian anti-Jewish polemic during the period under consideration, see, for example, Krauss 1996: 26-43; Williams 1935; Simon 1964; Wilken 1971; Wilken 1983; the contributions in Richardson – Granskou 1986; Taylor 1995; the contributions in Stroumsa – Limor 1996; Jacobs 2004:103-139; Fredriksen – Irshai 2006. For further documentary and archaeological evidence highlighting Jewish-Christian relations and controversies during this period, see, for example, the various contributions in Jacoby – Tsafrir 1988; Millar 1992; Millar 2004; Patrich 1995; Bar 2003. For arguments that the archaeological evidence in Byzantine Palestine demonstrates greater religious harmony, peaceful co-existence and cultural exchange between the local Jewish and Christian communities than evidenced in the contemporaneous written sources (but more problematic Christian-Samaritan interrelations), see Ribak 2007:14-21, 77-83; cf. Stemberger 2006:312-313.

[122] On contemporary (Ephraem Syrus and Gregory of Nazianzus) and later Christian reactions to Julian's plans to restore the Temple in Jerusalem, see Avi-Yonah 1984:194-205; Athanassiadi 1981:163, 165-166; Bowersock 1978: 88-89, 120-123; Lieu 1986:101-102; Smith 1996:192-197, 200, 203; Irshai 1999. For a summary of the archaeological history of the Temple Mount complex during its Christian pre-Islamic period, see now Kaplony 2002:23-28.

brought a deterioration of the Jews' legal status as the imperial government came to be engaged in a series of political, religious and military confrontations with Jewish communities and interests across his expanding Mediterranean empire. Consequently, some Jewish privileges from *Codex Theodosianus* were revoked and new anti-Jewish regulations were integrated in his *Codex Justinianus* of 529 which could amount to a direct intervention in the thus far unviolated religious autonomy of the Jews. Legal rhetoric in earlier imperial pronouncements had already introduced the term "superstition" (rather than "religion") with reference to Judaism,[123] and Justinian further undermined its legal recognition as a permitted religion by using both "superstition" and "heresy" in his anti-Jewish rhetoric, while trying also to achieve ecclesiastical authority over Jewish customs and observances.[124] This symptomatic permutation of legal rhetoric made it possible for future emperors to legitimize policies of the forcible conversion of Jews (in suitable religious and socio-political conditions), a trend reportedly started by Justinian himself with the forcible Christianization of a Jewish community in Borion, North Africa.[125]

Despite Justinian's infringements of Jewish internal and communal affairs, Byzantine Jews (unlike the Samaritans in this period) largely retained the core elements of their pre-Justinianian legal status. The same supersessionist theology in which Jewish "old Israel" was dethroned so that Christendom could be enthroned as the "true Israel"(visibly manifested in the God-ordained Christian empire), also viewed Jewry as the "living witness" for Christianity's inheritance of the Old Testament through the correct Christian interpretations of biblical prophecies as being fulfilled in the Gospel events. Jewry's continued, if enervated and vulnerable, existence under Christian supremacy was thus seen as a vital demonstration of its abandonment by God, whereas its further survival was seen as an imperative for the Second Coming.

---

123 On this terminological change and its implications, see Linder 1987:57f.

124 Generally on Justinian's anti-Jewish legislation and its implications, see Rabello 1987-88. On Justinian's superssesionist agenda behind the building of the *Nea Ekklesia* (the only church he erected in Jerusalem) intended to assimilate Christian perceptions of Salomon and the Temple to his imperial propaganda and image, see now Graham 2009.

125 Procopius, *De aedificiis*, 6.2.21-23 (ed. Haury – Wirth:4, 175).

Given the long history of Judaizing tendencies in Eastern Christianity, the Byzantine Church remained conscious of and strove to counter the attractions of Judaism to Christian heresies and heterodoxies, and to communities and individuals exhibiting (genuinely or allegedly) such tendencies, especially in areas like Phrygia. Nevertheless, the Byzantine Church also expected that Jews would gradually accept the truth of the Gospels through self-conscious choice and thus remained in principle opposed to the very concept of the forcible baptism of Jews. However, during times of internal upheavals and external military threats, such theological concerns could be overruled by the ideological and political agendas of the imperial government.

The early seventh century presented Byzantium with a series of such crises: its beginning brought internal turbulence and insecurity and until the failure of the planned Persian-Avaro-Slav joint attack and siege of Constantinople in 626 the empire found itself under sustained military pressure on the Balkan and eastern fronts. In such circumstances reports of Jewish support for the Sasanian invasion and occupation of Jerusalem was bound to put under strain the legal toleration of Byzantine treatment of the Jews and more relaxed secular or ecclesiastical attitudes to Judaism. A number of contemporaneous and later Christian sources allege a large-scale Jewish collaboration with the Persian invaders, ranging from welcoming and assisting them in certain areas to supporting them militarily and indulging in the burning of Christian churches and anti-Christian violence in Jerusalem.[126]

The extent to which these accounts can serve as trustworthy sources of such Jewish collaboration with the Persian armies and anti-Christian aggression has become of the most convoluted and controversial problems

[126] See, for example, Strategios, *La prise,* 8.17-18, 10; Strategios, *Expugnatio*, 8.17-18, 10; Sophronios, Anacreontica 14.105; Sebeos, 115; *Khuzistan Chronicle,* 26-27; Theophanes, *Chronographia,* 300-301; Eutychius, *Annalen*, 118-119. On the problem of the credibility of these reports, cf. Schäfer 1983:221-222; Wilken 1992:202-207, 218-232; Leder 1987:64-66; Flusin 1992:vol. 2, 162-164, 310f.; Dagron 1991:22-28; Schick 1994:20-48, *passim*; Olster 1994:79-84; Cameron 1994:80-82; Cameron 2002: *passim*; Fishman-Duker 1996:114-115.

related to the history of seventh-century Palestine.[127] To read these texts as authentic records of Jewish hostility to Christians and Christianity resulting from a supposed increase in Jewish-Christian animosities in Palestine prior to the Persian invasion would be certainly wrong. On the contrary, the archaeological data from excavated churches and synagogues of the Byzantine period suggest a largely peaceful co-existence and socio-cultural exchange between the Jewish and Christian communities in Palestine from the fifth to the seventh centuries (especially set against the background of the troublesome Christian-Samaritans inter-relations in the area).[128] It appears thus that the continuing and evolving inter-religious rivalries between the Christian and Jewish religious elites, which naturally intensified over the course of the multiplying anti-Jewish discriminatory measures of the imperial authorities, had a more limited impact on Jewish-Christian inter-communal relations on the ground in Byzantine Palestine than in other provinces of the empire.

On the other hand, it is hardly surprising that as Sassanid-Byzantine hostilities expanded into Palestine, the local Jewish communities may have reacted in accordance with their inherited and current pro-Persian sympathies. For these communities the Sassanid advance on Jerusalem inevitably evoked reminiscences of the events in 539-538 BCE when the Persian capture of Babylon under the founder of the Achaemenid monarchy, Cyrus the Great (559-530 BCE), led to the restoration of the exilic Jewish community to Jerusalem and Zion and the rebuilding and consecration of the Temple, completed under the patronage of Darius I the Great (521-486 BCE). The role of Persia in this paradigmatic Second Exodus (and First Return to Zion) was enshrined in the canonical books of Ezra and Nehemiah, and during the successive eras of Achaemenid, Parthian and Sassanid ascendancy in the Iranian world Irano-Jewish co-existence in the Near East was characterized by periods of close contacts, social and cultural exchange (including cases of ideological and political rapprochement) and far fewer conflicts and antagonisms than in Roman-Jewish relations. Later authoritative pronouncements from the rabbinic period could state that Rome was destined to be ultimately vanquished by Persia, although at the same

---

[127] On the modern historiographic debates and controversies regarding the reported Jewish anti-Byzantine alliances and collaboration with the invading Sassanid armies in Palestine, see Horowitz 1998; Cameron 1996:249-257.

[128] See Ribak 2007:14-21, 77-83. Cf. Stemberger 2006:312-313.

time, the advent of Messiah ben David could be expected only after a final brief period of the hegemony of the "evil" empire of Rome over the world.[129] Symptomatically, a tradition of utterances in aggadic midrashic literature (ascribed to no less a figure than the second century sage Simon ben Yohai) figuratively prophesized a future Persian military occupation/invasion of the Holy Land as foreshadowing the advent of the Messiah.[130]

At the same time, Jewish apocalyptic hostility to both pre-Christian and Christian Rome also had a venerable history and naturally intensified in periods of dramatic Roman-Jewish confrontation such as Hadrian's suppression of Bar Kokhba revolt in 132-135 CE. The imperial prohibitions and restrictions imposed on Jewish communities by the Christian Roman emperors in the Constantinian and immediate post-Constantinian periods deepened Jewish anti-Roman sentiments and provoked messianic reactions among some Jewish circles.[131] In general, Jewish perception of the Christian Roman empire continued to be dominated by the biblical typology identifying Rome with Israel's biblical antagonist, Edom, the violent and aggressive realm associated with Esau, "blessed" to live by the sword in Genesis 27:40.[132] Jewish historico-apocalyptic and eschatological readings of Daniel 7 also recognized Rome as the fourth kingdom of its schema which was to be ultimately overthrown and succeeded by the everlasting kingdom of the Israelite "holy ones of the Most High" (Daniel 7:27).

When within three years of the enthronement of Heraclius the seemingly unstoppable Persian advance reached Damascus and in the late spring of 614, Jerusalem, the Sasanian obliteration of Byzantine authority in Palestine predictably stirred messianic and eschatological sentiments among some local Jewish communities to whom the prophesied destruction and desolation of Edom (Isaiah 34; Jeremiah 49:7-11; Ezekiel 25:12-15; 35; Amos 1:11-13 and Obadiah 1), now incarnated in Byzantium, must have seemed to be approaching fast. It may be surmised from the sources for the Sasanian capture of Jerusalem that the Persian conquerors passed the Holy

---

129 Babylonian Talmud, Yoma 10a.

130 Lamentation Rabbati 1.13, Song of Songs Rabbah 8.10; see also Babylonian Talmud, Sanhendrin 98a.

131 See, for example, Van Bekkum 2002:97-98.

132 On Jewish perceptions of the Roman Empire and its associations with Edom and Esau, see De Lange 1978; De Lange 2005:418-420; van Bekkum 2002:101-103.

City to Jewish control or that the Jews came to enjoy initially a privileged status among its population but such a turn of events, while conceivable, remains conjecture.[133] Some circumstantial but inevitably abstruse evidence from the highly influential Jewish apocalyptic work *Sefer Zerubbabel*[134] and apocalyptic allusions in Jewish liturgical hymns from this period[135] suggest the resumption of some kind of Jewish cult observances and even sacrifices on the Temple Mount in the wake of the Persian annexation of Jerusalem. Any such Jewish attempts to resacralize and reclaim Judaism's holiest locus could have been only short-lived, as c. 617 the Persian pro-Jewish policies in the city were either overturned in favour of its more numerous Christian population or the Sasanian authorities chose to effect and maintain equilibrium between the two sides, initiating also the programme for the repair of city's Christian structures damaged during or after the takeover in 614.[136]

In *Sefer Zerubbabel*, moreover, the messianic and anti-messianic poles of the anticipated end-times conflict appear reversed vis-à-vis the Christian schema featuring a Jewish Antichrist. The apocalypse portrays a diabolized Roman world ruler, acting as a kind of an anti-Jewish Antichrist, who is

---

133 For the view that the Persian capture of Jerusalem was followed by a period of Jewish ascendancy in the city, see Baron 1957:22-23, 238-239n.25; Avi-Yonah 1984:265-269; Peters 1985:172-173; Peters 1986:87-88; Stemberger 1999:260; cf. also Van Bekkum 2002:103-104; for a balanced criticism of this view see Wilken 1992:212; Cameron 1994:80; Cameron 2002:63.

134 See the edition of one of the recensions of the apocalypse in Lévi 1914a:129-160; English translation in Himmelfarb 1990:67-90, and Reeves 2005:51-66. On the provenance of the historical allusions, eschatological and messianic notions in the apocalypse, cf. Israël Lévi's studies collected posthumously in Lévy 1994 and the subsequent occasionally differing views of Bamberger 1940; Wilken 1985:454-458; Wilken 1992:209-214; Berger 1985:141-164; Wheeler 1991:73-77; Dagron 1991:27ff., 41ff.; Stemberger 1999:266-269; Speck 1997:183-190; Dan 1998; Van Bekkum 1992:104-108; Himmelfarb 2002; Reeves 2005:40-51. For the related messianic and eschatological material in Sefer Eliahu (another Jewish apocalyptic work from the late Roman/early Byzantine period), see Krauss 1902; Wilken 1985:457-460; Wilken 1992:207-209; English translation in Reeves 2005:31-39.

135 The relevant liturgical hymns (*piyyutim*) have been published by Fleischer 1984-1985 and Yahalom 1979. On the apocalyptic and eschatological material in these *piyyutim*, see Yahalom 1996:278-280; Stemberger 1999:268-71; Sivan 2000; Van Bekkum 2002:108-110; Sivan 2004:81-91 *passim*.

136 Sebeos, 116-117; *Khuzistan Chronicle,* 26-27; see Howard-Johnston's critical scrutiny of the sources and their inconsistencies in Thomson – Howard-Johnston – Greenwood 1999:208-209; cf. Schick 1995:41.

named Armilos (a figure elaborated further in later Jewish literature), whose universal reign of terror tyrannizes “the holy people of the Most High”. Armilos is the final bellicose enemy of Nehemiah ben Hushiel, the Messiah son of Joseph and Menahem ben ʿAmiel, the Davidic Messiah – he kills the first in battle but is defeated and slain by the second. The most likely derivation of the name Armilos is a Hebraization of the Latin name of Rome's co-founder and paradigmatic king, “Romulus”, highlighting that the traditionally emphatic anti-Roman tenor of Jewish eschatological, messianic and restorationist speculations has been revived and heightened during the last Sasanian-Byzantine conflict. Some scholars have gone further, trying to find an actual historical identification of Armilos by treating the anti-Messianic Roman world conqueror as a personification of Heraclius, a theory which has attracted predictable criticism as resting on a too literal historical reading of the Jewish apocalypse.[137] Jewish perceptions of the Byzantine-Sasanian struggle apparently discerned also a characteristically Judaized religious dimension of its expansion to the Holy Land, recognizing it as battle between Jewry's long-standing oppressor, Edom (Rome/Byzantium), and its hereditary eastern imperial Persian rival, who was expected to initiate the revival of the Jewish cult in Jerusalem.[138]

With their intricate synthesis of historical allusion, biblical, messianic and eschatological material, *Sefer Zerubbabel* and the apocalyptically-oriented Jewish liturgical hymns of the period represent a problematic guide to the actual historical events and realities of Palestine during the first three decades of the seventh century. They reflect, however, through their historico-apocalyptic prism the dramatic religio-political and military vicissitudes of this period, including the Jewish disenchantment with the reversal of the Persian pro-Jewish stance in Jerusalem in 617. These documents shed light on the expectations that the Sasanian-Byzantine war and the Persian invasion of the Holy Land had inaugurated the eschatological age with its imminent conflicts, in which the two traditional Jewish messianic figures of the Messiah son of Joseph and Messiah son of David would confront Israel’s enemies to bring about the restoration of Jewish rule in Jerusalem, the renewal of the Temple cult and the establishment of Israel’s everlasting kingdom in the messianic age.

---

137 See the summary and criticism of the Armilos-Heraclius association in Dan 1998:93-94 n.56; cf. Reeves 2005:20-21.

138 See the analysis of Sivan 2004:88-90.

Such Jewish messianic expectations, triggered by the Sasanian caputure of Jerusalem, were naturally completely irreconcilable with the Byzantine vision and remoulding of Jerusalem as a parallel Christian capital of the empire,[139] as manifested by the unfolding of the extensive and prestigious building projects of churches and monasteries in and around the city since the dedication of the Church of the Holy Sepulchre in 335. Thus, apart from inflicting on Byzantium a major military and strategic crisis, the Sasanian occupation of Palestine and Jerusalem had serious repercussions on the ideological and religious plane. It presented a critical challenge to the Christian Roman triumphalist discourse of God-ordained imperial victory, as finding religio-political explanatory scenarios for the Byzantine defeat in the Holy Land in the face of the Sasanian armies continuing expansion of their conquests in imperial territory posed far more problems than any previous East Roman imperial predicament involving conflict with Sasanian Persia. The traditional attribution of defeats on the battlefield or natural calamities to the emperor's or citizens' sins now needed to be integrated into an interpretative framework that would seem more appropriate and persuasive in these new circumstances and for which the developing interaction and coalescence of crucial elements of the traditions of late Roman/Byzantine historical eschatology and imperial ideology could serve as a convenient source.

After the increasing eschatological concerns and speculations in Byzantium over the course of the sixth century,[140] the beginning of the Sasanian-Byzantine war in the early seventh century and its intensification following the enthronement of Heraclius, Šāhwarāz's capture of Jerusalem and the real threat of a Persian conquest of Constantinople brought a new intensity and pertinence to such eschatological trends.[141] The Sasanian takeover of Byzantine Palestine and Jerusalem thus did not only kindle Jewish-Christian strife in the Holy Land but activated the conflicting and mutually exclusive Jewish and Christian apocalyptic paradigms on the

---

139 On the notion of East Roman/Byzantine Jerusalem as a parallel Christian capital of the empire, see, for example, Dagron 1974:389; Jacobs:144-145.

140 See Alexander 1967:116-120; Scott 1985:107-109; Mango 1980:204-205; Magdalino 1993:5-11.

141 See, for example, *Life of Theodore of Sykeon*, 134 (ed. Festugière 1970:106); *Life of St George of Choziba,* 4.18 (ed. House 1888:117). For analysis of these trends, see Reinink 2002:82-83; Stroumsa 2008:289ff.

politico-eschatological plane, with their varying focus on the central end times role of the Holy City.

The canonical sources of this evolving synthesis of late Roman/early Byzantine eschatology and political theology comprised the eschatological teachings of the New Testament (developed further in the patristic period)[142] and selective use of Old Testament apocalyptic and eschatological material from Daniel and Ezekiel: the prophetic vision of the four successive world kingdoms in Daniel 2 and 7, the vision of the weeks in Daniel 9 and the prophecy of the onslaught of the northern allied hordes of Gog from the realm of Magog on the land of Israel in Ezekiel 38-39. Modern New Testament research has demonstrated the centrality of eschatology to the New Testament message and its intimate links with Second Temple Jewish apocalypticism and eschatology, in both its canonical and extracanonical sources and traditions. Millenarian trends in early Christianity such as Montanism and other related apocalyptic currents, seeking to revive apostolic Christianity and preoccupied with expectations of the forthcoming eschatological age, caused divisions and schisms. The end-time theologies of the early Church Fathers, which focused both on individual and universal eschatology, developed in a climate of intense apocalyptic speculations that was also affected by the continuing persecution of Christianity in the Roman empire and intense polemics with the theologians and leaders of the Gnostic schools who developed their own brands of Christian apocalypticism and eschatology.[143] Apocalyptic eschatology remained an important theological

---

[142] The so-called Apocalyptic Discourse in the synoptic gospels (Mark 13, Matthew 24-25 and Luke 21) and the Revelation (or Apocalypse) of John. These texts, as well as the apocalyptic notions developed, for example, in Colossians 1.20, 1 Corinthians 1.7 and 15.2, Corinthians 3, 5:1-5, 6:2 and 12:2ff., Galatians 1:12 and 1:16, Acts 22:17 and 22:23, 1 Thessalonians 4:13-18, Romans 1:17f. And 8:19-23 and Philippians 1:23, formed the New Testament core source material for early and medieval Christian apocalypticism and eschatology with their focus on the afterlife, the nature of heaven and hell, the Second Coming of Jesus Christ, the end of the world, the resurrection of the dead, the final judgment, the advent of the Messianic age and the institution of the Kingdom of God. On the New Testament Revelation of John as an "apocalyptic propaganda" intended to reinforce early Christianity's "sectarian stance" vis-à-vis Roman imperial ideology and its pressure on early Christian identity, see, for example, deSilva 1996.

[143] Themes such as eschatological salvation through the bodily resurrection of the dead were of central concern to Christian apologists like Irenaeus (c.130–c.200), Tertullian (c.160–c.225) and Clement of Alexandria (c.150–c.215), whereas the debates on the nature of Origen's (c.185–c.254), doctrines of the resurrection of the dead, punishment and

concern in patristic literature and its evolution and re-interpretations contributed crucially to major themes in Christian apocalypticism such as Antichrist lore, the chiliastic doctrine of the return of Christ to reign on earth for a millennium, speculations on the ages of the world which used different temporal patterns (world-weeks, etc.). The main eschatological tenets in both the Greek East and the Latin West found a normative basis in the eschatology-related statements of the Nicene creed regarding the Second Coming of Jesus Christ, the judgment of the living and the dead, the resurrection of the dead and ultimate establishment of the eternal Kingdom of God.[144]

Apart from the evolution of doctrinal patristic eschatology, the early Christian era witnessed the growth of another type of Christian apocalypticism manifested in new Christian apocalyptic pseudepigraphic writings as well as in Christian redactions of earlier Jewish apocalyptic pseudepigrapha. Some of these Christian apocryphal writings offered Christian versions of earlier Jewish "historical" apocalypticism, with its focus on the divinely predetermined course of history and its imminent eschatological crisis and end. During the fourth and fifth centuries in the Latin West Christian apocalypticism and chiliasm in the Latin West were challenged by major figures such as Jerome (c. 347–420) and Augustine (354-430) who elaborated what proved to be a highly influential non-apocalyptic theology of history and eschatology. However, the revival of the apocalyptic Sibylline traditions in the Greek East towards the end of the fourth century, as demonstrated by the emergence of the earliest Greek

damnation in afterlife and the final restoration of all things, aroused strong opposition and controversies. On the eschatological teachings of the early Church Fathers and the related doctrinal controversies of the patristic age, see, for example, Prete 1966; Daley 1991; Hill 1992; Heid 1993; Daley 2008.

144 The central eschatological beliefs in Eastern Orthodoxy were also integrated in the elaborate proceedings of Eastern Orthodox worship and prayer as manifested, for example, in the celebration of the Eucharist (see, for example, Louth 2008a:234-236). Eastern Orthodox beliefs and teachings in the sphere of individual eschatology crystallized after intense debate in the patristic period and occasionally continue to generate theological disputes. Eastern Orthodox eschatology rejects the notion of the existence of purgatory and considers it an unacceptable and late theological innovation. The history of the development of Eastern Orthodox eschatological teachings concerning the notions of eternal damnation and its character, the features of judgment in the afterlife, the characteristics of the resurrection bodies and the expected ultimate "restoration of all" still needs to be written.

("Theodosian") version of *Sibylla Tiburtina*,[145] showed that Christian apocalyptic eschatology and pseudepigraphy could assume new forms in which Christian salvation history and the destiny of the Christian Roman empire appear intrinsically interconnected.

The anti-apocalyptic attitudes of Jerome and Augustine led to the temporary discontinuing of the composition of new apocalyptic pseudepigrapha in the Latin West, although apocalyptic and eschatological notions and imagery continued to be circulated in epistles, homilies and commentaries such as Gregory the Great's *Homily on Ezekiel 2:6* and Beatus of Liébana's commentary on the Revelation.[146] In the Christian East the process of creating new pseudepigaphic apocalypses, however, continued into the early and high Middle Ages and East Christian historical apocalypticism was subjected to further revisions and elaborations and came to exercise a profound effect on the development of later medieval Western Christian apocalypticism.

Thus the composite corpus of late Roman/early Byzantine eschatology also came to include among its sources extra-canonical Christian and Jewish-Christian apocalyptic pseudepigrapha, the latter representing largely Christian redactions of earlier Jewish pseudepigraphic apocalypses, ranging from the early Christian to the early Byzantine period (all of which were still in circulation in the Christian East) as well as the revived apocalyptic Sibylline tradition (dependent on and re-working the genre of earlier Sibylline texts and historical apocalypses). Themes, imagery and protagonists from this flexible complex of traditions could coalesce in new eschatological prophecies, visions and pronouncements focused on the contemporaneous and future fortunes of the *imperium romanum christianum* and the succession of its emperors, updating inherited and borrowed eschatological material in accordance with the ever-changing historical circumstances.

---

[145] On the revival of the Sibylline tradition and the emergence of the earliest Greek version of the *Tiburtine Sibyl* in the late fourth century, see Alexander 1967; McGinn 1979:43-51; McGinn 1994:93-94. For the later Latin versions and manuscripts, see now the study of Holdenried 2004.

[146] On the apocalyptic material in these texts, see McGinn 1979:62-63, 77-79; on the somewhat differing patterns of the development of Christian apocalypticism in the Greek East and Latin West during this period, see McGinn 1975:252ff.

Beginning with Tertullian (c.160-220), earlier Christian exegesis of New Testament eschatological notions already recognized the Roman empire as the enigmatic *katechōn,* "restraining force" (2 Thessalonians 2:7-8), whose disappearance would set the stage for the eschatological manifestation of the Antichrist. The fourth and final world kingdom in Daniel 2 and 7, the one with legs of iron and feet of iron and clay which was to be replaced after the last judgment of the nations with the God-established universal and eternal kingdom of the "holy ones of the Most High" (Daniel 2:40-45, 7:9-28) predictably attracted continuous Christian eschatological interest. From the early patristic period onwards Christian interpretations of Daniel (and the resultant historico-apocalyptic schemes) commonly identified it with the Roman empire, a portrayal which could naturally generate largely pessimistic eschatological scenarios, especially in times of crises and political turbulence. Building on an exegetical trend initiated by the political theology of Constantine the Great's imperial apologist, Eusebius of Caesarea (c.260–c.340), other Byzantine (as well as some Syriac Christian) readings of the Danielic four kingdoms' historical incarnations advanced an alternative schema (on the basis of the millennial kingdom theme in Revelation 20:1-7) envisaging Christ's thousand-year reign on earth to be manifested through the Christian Roman empire which thus was to merge with the divinely-founded ultimate kingdom of the Danielic schema.[147] This latter Byzantine reading of Daniel 2 and 7 was naturally much more attuned to (and may have been promoted to) meet the needs of Byzantine imperial political theology in which, moreover, Christ was conceptualized as a co-emperor of the earthly emperor. It opened the way to imperial millenarian politics and manoeuvring, allowing also for continuous re-computations of eschatological and chiliastic events in circumstances either calling for such updated revisions of the future or in which they could be strategically useful.

---

[147] On these Byzantine readings of Daniel's four kingdoms scheme, see Podskalsky 1972, 11-12, 38-39; Podskalsky 1984, 440-442; Magdalino 1993, 10-11, 25-26; Reinink 2002, 81-95, at 83-84 (and the more optimistic imperial eschatology which remained based on the recognition of the Danielic fourth kingdom as the Roman empire in the *Syriac Alexander Legend*, discussed in Reinink 200:85-86). Podskalsky 2004. On Cosmas Indicopleustes' interpretation of the Roman empire as transcending the Danielic four kingdoms' scheme and as representing the eternal kingdom established by the God of heaven, as prophesized in Daniel 2:44 (*Christian Topography*, 2.lxix-lxxv), see also Casey 1989. For parallel attempts in Syriac Christianity to associate the Christian Roman empire with the Danielic everlasting kingdom and the eschatological kingdom of Christ (Aphrahat and Ephraem Syrus), see further Podskalsky 1972, 15-16; Griffith 1986; Morrison 2004.

Given the centrality of Jerusalem and the Holy Land to the inherited and evolving Christian historico-eschatological scenarios, the religiously tumultuous events related to its Sasanian capture and the subsequent (if short-lived) Jewish ascendancy allowed for updates and re-interpretations of these scenarios in which the Persians and the Jews can appear not only as religious but apocalyptic enemies of Christendom. In the case of the Jewish allies of the Sasanian conquerors of the Holy Land, Jewish ambitions to reclaim and re-sanctify the Temple Mount in the aftermath of the capture of Jerusalem was bound to be seen as reminiscent of apocalyptic and Antichrist traditions developed during the patristic period around New Testament eschatological material and imagery in passages referring, for example, to the "Abomination of Desolation" (*to bdelugma tēs erēmōseōs*), dwelling in the holy place (Matthew 24:15) and the "man of sin", "the son of perdition" (*ho anthropos tēs anomias, ho huios tēs apoleias*), taking his seat in the Temple of God (2 Thessalonians 2:2-4), elaborated with notions such as the Antichrist's postulated Jewish and tribe of Dan pedigree.[148] Portrayals of the Persian conquerors of the Holy Land as religious enemies of Christianity could draw on the panoply of inherited East Roman anti-Persian stereotypes and polemical cliches about Zoroastrianism and its cultic observances such fire-veneration, etc. The fall of Jerusalem was also presented in a providential framework: the Persian conquerors could have been depicted as "evil beasts", "mad dogs" and "ferocious serpents," but their fire and sword was intended to cleanse the impurity bred by the sins of its inhabitants.[149]

But apart from such predictable explanatory frameworks, one of the principal thrusts of Byzantine anti-Sasanian propaganda after 614 was to present the Sasanian monarchy as the principal adversary of Christendom, aggressively bent on its destruction and accordingly the damage done to Christian ecclesiastical compounds and the loss of human life during Jerusalem's capture were heavily hyperbolized to assume the proportion of a monumental crime against Christianity.[150] The Sasanian seizure of the True Cross from the Church of the Holy Sepulchre and its recovery at the end of the war were given a prominence in the framework of what was largely

[148] On the development of the Antichrist tradition in the early Christian and patristic periods, see Bousset 1895; Heid 1993; McGinn 1994:45-79; Badilita 2005.

[149] Cf. Strategius, *Expugnatio* (Arabic version C), 6:9-11; Sophronius, *Anacreontica*, 18:25.

[150] On the accounts of the Persian conquest of Jerusalem as a main current of Byzantine anti-Sasanian propaganda, see Howard-Johnston 1996:36-37; Howard-Johnston 2004:102-103.

presented as a Zoroastrian-Christian religious confrontation. The intention of Heraclius' speeches to his Byzantine troops reported in Theophanes' *Chronographia* was clearly intended to mobilize their Christian fervour, dwelling, for example, on the anti-Christian outrages of the "enemies of God' who had trampled on imperial land, burnt Christian sanctuaries, profaned altars and defiled churches.[151] In another speech (reported to have been delivered upon his incursion into Sasanian territory in 623), Heraclius calls upon his troops to avenge the insult Xusraw II had done to God and inspired by faith, fight bravely the adversary who, "armed with impiety", has inflicted much terrible suffering on the Christians.[152] The speech is completed with the emperor's "promise" that encountering danger is not without "recompense" but would lead to "eternal life",[153] a notion taken further in a later address to his soldiers during a particularly difficult stage of the campaign, in which he appeals to his soldiers to sacrifice themselves to God for the salvation of their brothers.[154] Through this self-sacrifice in battle they would win the "crowns of martyrdom", receive future praise and "recompense from God". The significance of the Christian military-religious ideology underlying the Byzantine war effort is emphasized by references to the religious services performed by his armies at various stages of the campaign;[155] the emperor declares that his army is under God's protection[156] and divine intervention assists Byzantine progress and victories over the Persian armies.[157]

In the Byzantine propaganda-related material in the accounts of the Byzantine-Sasanian hostilities (which included disinformation and ascribing to Xusraw II concocted anti-Christian statements in official imperial communications) the Sasanian monarch is castigated as a *kosmolethron*, "destroyer of the world",[158] "God-abhorred and execrated", an "opponent of

[151] Theophanes, *Chronographia,* 303.12-304.13 (for the speech, its background and aftermath in the context of Byzantine anti-Persian campaign preparations).
[152] Theophanes, *Chronographia,* 307.3-6.
[153] Theophanes, *Chronographia,* 307.10-11.
[154] Theophanes, *Chronographia,* 310.25-311.2.
[155] Theophanes, *Chronographia,* 308.14-15; 320.11-12.
[156] Theophanes, *Chronographia,* 310.26-27; 317.18-21.
[157] Theophanes, *Chronographia,* 310.10-13; 318.17-20.
[158] Theophanes, *Chronographia*, 308.25.

God", who blasphemes against Jesus Christ, the Virgin Mary[159] and the True Cross,[160] etc. The diabolized, anti-Christian image of Xusraw II was taken to its furthest extreme in the contemporaneous panegyrical works of George of Pisidia which, drawing on a rich array of biblical and classical themes and imagery, praised and depicted Heraclius' epic military struggle with Sasanian Persia in explicitly religious terms (with an intense anti-Zoroastrian rhetoric)[161] and elevated it to a cosmic level battle against sin and Satan, both typified in Xusraw.[162] Characteristically, drawing on biblical typologies, George of Pisidia compares Xusraw's profanation of Christendom's shrines and religion in Jerusalem in 614 to the sacrilege of Belshazzar, the son and co-regent of the last king of Babylon, Nabonidus, who profaned in his feast the sacred vessels of the First Temple, brought from Jerusalem after its conquest by Nebuchadnezzar (Daniel 5:1-4).[163]

At the same time, the providential framework in which traditionally Byzantine military defeats and setbacks were interpreted as God's punishment for Byzantine sins, they could also be seen as crucial stages in the unfolding of the God-guided eschatological drama determining the fortunes of the universal empire. The earlier East Roman – Persian war of 502-506 had already stirred eschatological expectations, reflected in the new expanded version of the *Tiburtine Sibyl*,[164] thus the notion that a major military conflict between the two imperial rivals would inaugurate the era of the Last Days had been already in circulation in apocalyptic circles in the Christian East. There are clear indications that apart from the use of intense anti-Sasanian religious rhetoric, an exploitation of historico-apocalyptic notions to create such eschatological schemes was part of the politico-

---

159 *Chronicon Paschale,* 728 (a dispatch regarding the dethronement of Xusraw which is attributed to Heraclius and reportedly read out from the pulpit in Constantinople's patriarchal basilica of Hagia Sophia in May 628).

160 George of Pisidia, *In Restitutionem Sanctae Crucis*, 64-68 (ed. Pertusi 1959:228).

161 See, for example, George of Pisidia, *Expeditio Persica* 2.249-255, 368-75; 3.1-6.

162 George of Pisidia, *Expeditio Persica*; George of Pisidia, *In Restitutionem Sanctae Crucis*; George of Pisidia, *Heraclias.* On George of Pisidia's presentation of the Byzantine-Persian war in emphatically religious terms, see Frendo 1986:53-62; Olster 1991; Olster 1994:51-72 *passim*; Whitby 1998:253-254; Whitby 2002; Haldon 1999:20-21; Huber 2008:162-192; Howard-Johnston 2010:ch.1, 16-36 *passim*. See also the discussion of the presentation of the last Byzantine-Sassanid war as a struggle between Christianity and Zoroastrianism, waged with a "holy war" ethos, in the *Khuzistan Chronicle* in Watt 2002:67-72.

163 George of Pisidia, *Heraclias*, 1.30-34.

164 Alexander 1967.

military agenda of Heraclius' court during the last two phases of the war. This is particularly evident in the efforts to link the rule and Persian campaigns of Heraclius with those of Alexander the Great through the literary medium of apocalyptic prophecies as evidenced in the Syriac *Alexander Legend* (c. 630).[165] Clearly intended to portray Heraclius as a "new Alexander," this work was certainly composed to furnish further ideological validity for Heraclius' designs to secure and strengthen the loyalty of the non-Chalcedonian communities in his restored empire and bring them again into communion with the Byzantine Chalcedonian church.[166] This work also testifies to important elements of the political theology underpinning Heraclius' ceremonial reclaiming of Jerusalem as the Holy City of Christendom in 630 in which the reinstatement of the True Cross was also meant to re-affirm (after the loss and recovery of the Holy Land) the inextricable link between Christ's heavenly kingship and Roman Christian emperorship. The two apocalyptic prophecies (the first of which is associated with Alexander and the second with the Persian king, Tubarlaq) in the *Syriac Alexander Legend* are clearly linked to the distinct religious and eschatological themes of the imperial propaganda devised to address the struggle with and victory over Sasanian Persia in the 620s, forecasting the ultimate downfall of Persia and its kings and the end times assimilation of all earthly sovereignty and the imperial office itself by Christ. Symptomatically, these prophecies extol the Roman empire as the legitimate heir to the kingdom of the "house of Alexander" which will endure until the last days when it will submit the earthly kingdom to Christ, for whose Second Coming and enthronement Alexander bequeathed his royal throne and crown to Jerusalem.[167]

An apocalyptic prophecy predicting the final Roman victory over the Persians before the Last Days and attributed to Xusraw II appears also in Theophylact Simoccata's *History* which was written during Heraclius' reign.[168] Employing an apocalyptic hebdomad periodization, the author behind this "Xusraw" prophecy envisages three hebdomads of Babylonian

---

165 *Syriac Alexander Legend* (ed. Budge 1889).

166 For the date and the religio-political *raison d'être* of the work, see Reinink 1985; Reinink 2002; Reinink 2003, esp. 151-165.

167 *Syriac Alexander Legend*, ed. Budge 1889:257-258, 270, 275 (text); 146-147, 270, 275 (translation).

168 Theophylact Simocatta, *History*, 5.15.5-7 (ed. De Boor 1887:216-217).

(Persian) supremacy over the Romans, followed by a Roman triumph over the Persians in the final hebdomad which sets the stage for the dissolution and end of the transient world.[169] When viewed against the background of the already quoted Jewish eschatological pronouncements of the rabbinic period, envisaging an end-time struggle between the Roman and Persian empires before the advent of the final messianic kingdom, these apocalyptic prophecies forged in Byzantine wartime propaganda inevitably develop the scenario of a Roman victory setting the stage for the advent of the eternal kingdom of Christ. Theophylact Simoccata's *History* suggests, moreover, that Sasanian wartime propaganda may have used a similar Alexander-related prophetic technique for its own purposes: the text ascribes to Xusraw II claims that he had a vision of the Virgin Mary who predicted that he would be granted the victories of Alexander the Great.[170] These claims may well reflect Sasanian political propaganda from the time of the Persian conquests targeting the Christian population of the occupied Byzantine territories and aiming to assure them of the divine sanction for their superseding of the imperial Christian order with a non-Christian Persian rule.[171] This particular prophecy lacks the eschatological dimension of the wartime politico-apocalyptic Byzantine prophecies but may throw a fascinating light on the possible use of the prophetic medium by Sasanian propagandist irredentism to legitimize its authority in annexed Byzantine provinces through a prediction of Sasanian conquests as a reversal of those of Alexander, ascribed, moreover, to a paradigmatic Christian figure.[172]

The development and exploitation of Byzantine wartime religious and apocalyptic rhetoric and imagery after 614, with their portrayals of Xusraw II and his bellicose Sasanian empire as the ultimate enemy of Christendom, were clearly intended to mobilize the total support and spiritual resources of the Christians of the beleaguered empire[173] but were also intended to win over the Christian subjects of Sasanian Persia, particularly in Transcaucasia, and there various strands of evidence reveal that this tactic was at least

---

[169] On the links between the apocalyptic hebdomad periodization of the "Xusraw" prophecy and the chronology of Byzantine-Sasanian relations since the late sixth or early seventh centuries, cf. Whitby 1988:240-241; Whitby – Whitby (transl.) 1986:153 n.80, 81; Reinink 2002:87-89.

[170] Theophylact Simocatta, *History*, 5.15.8-11 (ed. De Boor 1887:217).

[171] See the analysis of Whitby – Whitby (transl.) 1986:154 n.83; Reinink 2002:89-90.

[172] On some aspects of Xusraw II internal religio-political propaganda, see Daryaee 1997.

[173] See, for example, Whitby 1998:194.

partially successful.[174] Elaborating this anti-Christian image of Xusraw II in Byzantine propaganda targeting the Sasanians' long-standing Christian subjects (and those in the Persian-occupied imperial territories) was particularly relevant in the framework of Xusraw II's well attested interest in Christianity[175] (which may have possibly provoked the suspicions of the Zoroastrian clergy)[176] and (at least until the final years of his reign) his tolerant, neutral and pragmatic policy in striving to strike a balance between the Nestorian and Monophysite communities in Sasanian Persia.[177]

Furthermore, while taking advantage of Sasanian dynastic strife and court factionalism in the wake of Xusraw's dethronement in 628, Heraclius' designs on Persia (he is praised in Theophanes as a "saviour even of Persia")[178] may have included the Christianization of its weakened Zoroastrian monarchy and divided aristocracy (although the evidence for such designs remains circumstantial)[179] with whom he negotiated the recovery of the of the True Cross, "the treasure of the whole world," as well as other church relics.

The religious, symbolic and ideological significance of the subsequent restoration of the "glorious and precious" True Cross to the Church of Holy Sepulchre by Heraclius was reinforced with further religio-political acts intended to highlight the emperor's hard-won stature and image as a saviour of Christendom, the Holy Land, Jerusalem and its most precious shrines and relics. Elaborating with carefully constructed biblical and classical typologies (and a linked rich array of exempla, allusions and metaphors) the image of Heraclius as a model Christian ruler and warrior, his imperial propagandist, George of Pisidia, compares his entry into Jerusalem to

---

[174] See, for example, Howard-Johnston 1999:37-39; Howard-Johnston 2004:103-104.

[175] Theophylact Simocatta, *History*, 4.10.2-4; 5.13.4-6, 14.2-11,15.8-11. On Xusraw's interest and dedications to the cult of St Sergius, for example, see Whitby 1988:234-236, 239, 298, 300, 305; Fowden 1999:134-167.

[176] Shahîd 2004:229-231.

[177] See the up-to-date analyses in Greatrex 2003; Panaino (forthcoming).

[178] Theophanes, *Chronographia*, 308.25.

[179] For the evidence suggesting such designs, see Frolow 1953; Mango 1985. Cf. the more recent analyses of the relevant events in Whittow 1996:80-81; Kaegi 2003:181-182, 187-188; Panaino 2004:824-834; Panaino 2010. Cf. the reservations concerning such designs in Frendo 2000:38-39.

restitute the True Cross with Jesus Christ's arrival in the holy city on Palm Sunday. The "triumphant" cross is itself likened to the Ark of the Covenant because of its power to overpower its adversaries and is extolled as the holy weapon with which the "emperor with God's aid" finally vanquished Khosroes who had blasphemed against it.[180] In George of Pisidia's *Heraclias*, God's own work in the first six days of creation can be paralleled in the six years of Heraclius' campaigning against Sasanian Persia, whereas the seventh day of rest is reflected in the victory and peace which the emperor achieved in the seventh year of his counter-offensive.[181] Heraclius's exploits were thus extolled with eschatological imagery: his reinstatement of imperial and Christian victory over Persia amounted to a renewal and recreation of the world, inaugurating a new era, which makes him a worthy bearer of the titles "commander of the cosmic rebirth" and *kosmorystēs* ("saviour of the world").[182]

The progression and route of Heraclius' religio-political displays following his victory in Persia, which culminated in his advent in Jerusalem (and he was extolled as the first Christian Roman emperor to enter the "Holy City" in living memory)[183] suggest not only a dedicated campaign of imperial restoration of the Constantinian model but also a conscious imperial millenarian agenda. In 629 he formally adopted the Greek *basileus* (which earlier had acquired its full royal significance through its use by Alexander the Great and his Hellenistic successors) as his main imperial title in a Christianized version of "faithful *basileus* in Christ", overshadowing the traditional Latin *imperator Caesar Augustus*. Heraclius thus became the first Christian Roman emperor to invoke the name of Christ in his titulature to legitimize his imperial dignity, revealing a new enhanced focus on the emperor's divine election and the inextricable unanimity of the spiritual heavenly monarchy and its earthly replica, the Byzantine empire. Heraclius' revision of imperial titulature in the wake of the Persian wars, with their perceived and overtly declared religious significance (at least on the

---

180 George of Pisidia, *In Restitutionem Sanctae Crucis*, 27-38, 54-60, 64-68 (ed. Pertusi 1959:226-228; ed. Tartaglia 1998:253-255).

181 This particular part of George of Pisidia's *Heraclias* is preserved in Theophanes, *Chronographia*, 327-328.

182 George of Pisidia, *Heraclias*, 1.65-70, 201-206. On this portrayal of Heraclius by George of Pisidia, see, for example, Olster 1991:161-162; Whitby 1994:206; Whitby 1998:254, 260.

183 See the anonymous "Return of the Relics of the Holy Martyr Anastasios the Persian from Persia to his Monastery" in Flusin 1992:1, 99.

Byzantine side) betrays also a stronger emphasis on Old Testament Davidic royal ideology, as appropriated and refashioned in Byzantine imperial political theology, and a possible eschatological orientation.[184] Indeed the timing of Heraclius' restoration of the True Cross to Jerusalem and the manner in which it was enacted and propagated in Byzantium (with all the inevitable miracle stories that came to be associated with the event) can been interpreted as "a deliberate apocalyptic act",[185] best understood in the framework of a "realized eschatology"[186] in the dawning new imperial era (itself, one of the central messages of imperial propaganda) when the expected Second Coming would initiate the joint rule of Christ and the "faithful *basileus* in Christ" over the empire which was finally to be assimilated to the eschatological thousand-year kingdom.

Concerted efforts were made, moreover, to associate Heraclius' restoration of imperial order and victorious wars in the name of Christianity with the analogous deeds of Constantine the Great, bringing to the fore the message of imperial renewal and the re-establishment of Constantine's Christian empire. While following the Christianization of the Roman empire the East Roman/Byzantine emperor was in principle conceptualized as a "new David" and "new Constantine", Heraclius' reign re-focused on the use of the Constantinian cult and nomenclature in a more significant and pointed way, triggering a "Constantinian" momentum in the imperial ideology and propaganda of his own Heraclian, as well as succeeding Byzantine dynasties between the seventh and tenth centuries. Building on the Constantinian model of Christian emperorship, Heraclius' programme of imperial renewal was intertwined with his energetic endeavours in the 630s to achieve religious uniformity and ecclesiastical unification in the empire in view of the antagonism between the Byzantine Chalcedonian Orthodox church establishment and the non-Chalcedonian Monophysite communities in the regained eastern provinces.

---

[184] See, for example, Shahîd 1972:302f. (according to Shahid the adoption of the title may have been related to Heraclius' hopes that "he was opening the last phase of the millennium as a *praeparatio* for the Second Coming," Shahîd 1972: 308); Cf. Alexander 1977:232-233; Magdalino 1993:19. Generally, on the ideological and theological connotations of Heraclius' assumption of the title of *basileus* see also Dagron 2003:28-29.

[185] Mango 1990:205; Cf. Flusin 1992:2, 214-215; Magdalino 1993:18-19; Drijvers 2002:186-88.

[186] Magdalino 1994:9; Magdalino 1993:10-11, 19; Flusin 1992:214-215; Whitby 1992:73; Reinink 2002:83-84; Drijvers 2002: 187-188.

Following the traumatic loss of Palestine to Xusraw II's armies in 614 and their recovery after 628, Jerusalem and the Holy Land were naturally anticipated to play a vital role in the thus inaugurated new imperial age and Heraclius sponsored and secured further finance for the completion of the repairs of the damaged Christian sacral architecture in the "Holy City". It has been argued, moreover, that Heraclius planned and embarked on building projects at the Temple Mount complex intended to repossess it for Christianity in the new religio-political conditions after the fall of Jerusalem, the interlude of the Jewish ascendancy there and the city's Byzantine recovery.[187] While finding some support in circumstantial evidence, these arguments have not been corroborated as yet by solid archaeological data and their assumptions need to be tested by further archaeological investigations. Later Christian traditions recounting Heraclius' erection of or entry through the Temple Mount's Golden Gate or building activities in the abandoned area of the destroyed second Temple area seem to reflect popular Christian pilgrims' lore which acquired new relevance in the context of the Christianization of the complex in the wake of the First Crusade (1095-1099) and the establishment of the Latin Kingdom of Jerusalem.[188]

Finally, Heraclius' restitution of the True Cross had an anti-Judaic potential which was promptly put to use by him during his stay in Jerusalem and its aftermath. In the eschatologically loaded atmosphere in which Heraclius celebrated the re-assertion of Byzantine authority over Jerusalem and the Holy Land, the real and perceived Jewish role in the Persian conquest seemed bound to have repercussions for the immediate fortunes of the communities in the empire. Heraclius' first reactions to rising Jewish-Christian inter-confessional tensions (as Persian forces were withdrawing from Syria and Palestine) and reported outbursts of Christian anti-Jewish violence do not seem to indicate that initially he followed a conscious and

---

[187] Peters 1986:87-89, 95, 119 n.54; Peters 1983:119-138. For arguments that the extant archaeological and historical evidence makes Heraclius the likely builder of the Golden Gate to the Temple Mount, see Mango 1992; Bahat 1999:254-256; for arguments that the Golden Gate was built in the late Byzantine period and restored during the latter part of Heraclius' war against the Sassanids, see Creswell 1969:1, 317-318.

[188] See, for example, some of the medieval Christian descriptions of visits to Jerusalem and its monuments assembled in Peters 1985:302, 315 and 320.

systematic anti-Judaic agenda.[189] However, following his restoration of the cross in Jerusalem, Heraclius' policies and attitudes to the Jewish communities of Jerusalem and the Holy Land hardened and he reportedly allowed or authorized violent repressions against the Jews in Jerusalem who were subsequently expelled again from the Holy City.[190] In 632 Heraclius' anti-Jewish measures reached their culmination when in a landmark edict he decreed the forcible conversion of all Jews in the empire.[191]

Heraclius' decree was clearly conditioned by the new religio-political realities and concerns shaped in the aftermath of his Persian wars such as his attempts to enforce the religious centralization of the empire and the imperial government's rising suspicions of Jewish loyalty to the Christian empire and readiness to collaborate with its external enemies. These suspicions deepened during the recent wars with Persia and the Sasanian threat to Byzantium's eastern provinces, a threat that was to be supplanted in the 630s by the swiftly escalating menace of the Muslim-Arab conquests in the Near East. Imperial Christian anti-Judaism was further reinforced by the new sense of the magnitude of Jewish-Christian rivalries over the Holy Land and Jerusalem, as re-defined during and after the Constantinian period and intensified during the recent Sasanian occupation of Palestine and the brief period of Sasanian-instituted Jewish sway in the Holy City.

The polemical and hagiographic genres of Byzantine Christian literature presented characteristic narratives of Jewish conversions to Christianity, some of which may have reflected actual occurrences but on the whole were meant to maintain the conviction in Christianity's supersession of Judaism. This theological supersessionism could be incorporated in learned and

---

189 On Heraclius' policies towards the Jews during the initial period of his stay in the Holy Land and before his arrival in Jersualem, cf. Avi-Yonah 1984:270-271; Sharf 1955:101-102; Cameron 2002:64-65.

190 Theophanes, *Chronographia*, 328:24-28; Eutychius, *Annales*, 129.

191 The decree is referred to in the chronicle of Michael the Syrian, *Chronique* (ed. Chabot 1899-1910:2, 414; plays a significant role in the anti-Judaic polemical work, *Doctrina Jacobi nuper baptizati* (ed. Déroche 1991) and is discussed in a letter written by Maxiumus Confessor in 632 (ed. Devréesse 1937). The authenticity of the passage referring to Heraclius' decree in Maximus Confessor's letter is questioned by some scholars – cf. the views of Starr 1940:192-196; Dagron 1991:30f.; Laga 1990:183-188; Speck 1997:441-467; Brandes 1992:38-39.

popular Christian end-time beliefs and speculations in which the ultimate Jewish conversions to Christianity accordingly could be expected to take place in the eschatological age. Thus it does not seem coincidental that Heraclius' anti-Jewish decree followed on and effectively served as the concluding deed of a series of public imperial acts which appear to have been intended to enact (or to be seen as enacting) an eschatological scenario, all the more that two of the later Byzantine emperors who re-enacted the decree, Leo III (717-741) and Basil I (867-886), also shared to some extent his eschatological preoccupations.[192]

The Christian ideology underlying the Byzantine war effort during the lengthy military conflict with Sasanian Persia between 603-628 and its religious dimension show some inevitable continuities but also some striking innovations against the background of earlier Roman hostilities with the Sasanian monarchy and their religious aspects. Elements of the inherited military-religious ideology such as God-guidedness in battle and imperial triumphalism, religious services in the army, belief in divine interventions which will strike the adversary and so on, were naturally retained and on occasions intensified. The tradition of clerical figures taking an active part in the organization of defensive warfare was also retained and found an impressive manifestation when during the great joint siege of Constantinople by the Persians and the Avars in 626, the Constantinople Patriarch Sergios I acted as regent in the absence of Emperor Heraclius and was in charge of defence. A contemporary homily reflects the patriarch's public statements during the siege, which, moreover, carry the discernible overtones of a religious war, proclaiming that God Himself will fight for Constantinople's citizens.[193] In an atmosphere permeated with religious enthusiasm, sustained with military religious rites and ceremonies, the patriarch used the image of the Virgin Mary to threaten the foreign and "devilish" armies with her supernatural martial protection of the city. As anticipated and proclaimed by the patriarch, during the crisis she defends her city and chases away the Avar khagan, who concedes his inevitable defeat to the Mother of God.

But it is the extent to which religious agendas, themes, imagery and actual goals came to dominate the imperial discourse on the war and the

---

192 See the analysis in Magdalino 1994:8-9; Magdalino 1993:20, 24.

193 On these episodes during the siege of Constantinople and the quoted homily of Theodore Synkellos, see Cameron 1979:20–21.

resultant propaganda efforts which certainly has no precedent in previous East Roman-Sasanian hostilities. The Sasanian capture of the Holy Land, Jerusalem and the True Cross provided the imperial government with the pretext to portray the Sasanian adversaries as implacable enemies of Christendom and greatly magnify the religious dimension of the warfare, aiming to procure the support of the Christian communities in the Sasanian realm, especially in the Transcaucasian areas which had traditionally been contested spheres of influence between the two empires. The reports of the alleged massive destruction and conflagration of the Christian sacral architecture of Jerusalem and the slaughter and deportation of its Christian population were used to inspire Christian ardour, especially among the imperial troops who were given to understand that they were facing a religious enemy who had conquered, destroyed and defiled Christendom's holiest places. Calling for self-sacrifice, Heraclius went as far as to promise military martyrdom and heavenly rewards (recompense from God) to imperial Christian soldiers who fell in the battle for the salvation of their Christian brothers against the Christendom's main adversaries. As already mentioned, the articulation of the notion of heavenly recompense for fallen Christian soldiers in a speech attributed to the Roman army commander Justinian, supposedly delivered in 576, may well actually reflect Heraclius' related rhetoric of heavenly reward for martial self-sacrifice, being projected back by Theophylact Simocatta to an earlier Persian-Roman military engagement.

This clearly demonstrates that the idea of Christian warriors as martyrs for Byzantine Orthodoxy, fighting for the salvation of their souls and their brothers, as articulated during the reign Nikephoros Phokas had its roots in the new Christian ideology of warfare which took shape during Heraclius' counter-offensive against Sasanian Persia in the 620s. Perhaps Nikephoros Phokas' revival of the notion was part of a trend in Byzantine military religious ideology which may have been encouraged more frequently by the imperial court than the extant recorded cases indicate. This may suggest certain continuities in the ethics and martyrology of Byzantine Christian warfare which possibly can be traced to the Anatolian frontier zones of the empire and to Heraclius' innovative declarations concerning the promise of military martyrdom for his troops fighting the Persian "enemies of God". The intriguing suggestion that this notion of Christian military martyrdom can be traced further back to mid-fifth century Armenia (as indicated by *The History of Lazar P'arpets'i*)[194] and thus could find ready recipients among

[194] Howard-Johnston 1999:40, in reference to *The History of Lazar P'arpets'i* (transl. Thomson 1991, 111-117, 190-193, 201). On the notion of martyrdom on the battlefield in

Heraclius' Armenian auxiliaries could open a fruitful line of inquiry, tracing its roots to a period of Armenian religious strife and religiously motivated military conflict with Sasanian Persia.

Apart from its heightened religious rhetoric, Heraclius' counter-offensive had some more or less openly stated actual religious goals as part of its imperial politico-military agenda, given, among other things, the prominence assigned to the recovery of the True Cross in wartime propaganda and peace negotiations in the aftermath of Xusraw II's dethronement. As a result the ideology of Byzantine anti-Persian warfare under Heraclius blends notions of the inherited just war tradition with some elements of religious war, finding inevitably scriptural legitimation in the biblical wars and warrior figures fighting in the name of God. Moreover, it was not only the Sasanian regime but Zoroastrianism itself, which was frequently depicted as an adversary of Roman imperial Christianity, whose shrines appeared a legitimate target, especially after the Sasanian takeover of Jerusalem when the Persian invaders were charged in written and verbal propaganda with anti-Christian atrocities and devastation of Christianity's holy places. The widespread Christian anguish (at least in imperial territories) caused by the fall of Jerusalem could be consequently augmented by a sense of outrage at the perceived grievous sacrileges committed by the Sasanian conquerors (and their Jewish allies). The Sasanian conquest of Jerusalem thus played a crucial role in the panoply of religiously-charged themes intended to reinforce the religious aspect of the anti-Persian warfare. It is worth adding that a kind of a *ius in bello* prohibition (not systematically observed) on the destruction of sacral sites/temples and sacrilege existed in Graeco-Roman antiquity,[195] so the notion of Sasanian desecration and conflagration of Jerusalem's Christian sacral architecture also allowed for the further symbiosis of traditional Graeco-Roman just war notions with those of a Christian *bellum sacrum*. Much of this propaganda effort was directed at the non-Chalcedonian Christian groups under Sasanian sovereignty (as well as and especially in contested spheres of influence in Transcaucasia where it seems to have been successful); indeed it can be seen as the culmination of East Roman/Byzantine endeavours to earn the religious, and ultimately, political allegiance of these communities.

However, these religious features and aims, the association with Jerusalem and the Holy Land, or the manner of conducting of the campaigns

---

fifth-century Armenia, see also Thomson 2004:377-378. Heraclius' possible Armenian descent (Shahîd 1972:310; Kaegi 2003:21) may well be relevant in this context.

[195] See the analysis of this veto on sacrilege in Grant 1980:184-187.

are not sufficient to define Heraclius' Persian wars as a "crusade" when the term is used in its specific religio-military sense and not simply as a metaphor. Their mechanical labeling as a 'crusade' or 'proto-crusade' can obscure the serious differences between the legitimization and conduct of Heraclius' inter-imperial military conflict with Sasanian Persia and the Jerusalem/Holy Land campaigns of the crusading movement, with their specific theoretical basis (which came to incorporate features of the Augustinian just war model), as well as their ideological and legal frames conditioned by the various patterns of religious change in eleventh-twelfth centuries Western Christendom and the papacy's role in and response to them. These Western Christian religious, political and legal contexts are not applicable to contemporaneous Byzantium, even less to Heraclius' beleaguered early seventh-century empire, hence his campaigns could not have served as a vehicle for ecclesiastical militarism or as a "penitential act of religious votaries".[196] Significantly, the heightened religious sentiments and elements in Heraclius' campaigns (some of which were shaped in reaction to the Sasanian conquest of Jerusalem) did not mature and crystallize during his Persian wars, the subsequent Muslim Arab invasions, or after his reign vis-a-vis the massive religio-political challenges posed by the reign of the Caliphate into a consistently and systematically developed theory of a Christian holy war comparable to that in the Latin West during the crusading era. The notion of military martyrdom and heavenly rewards for martial self-sacrifice also vanish (at least from the records) until its attempted but unsuccessful revival by Nikephoros Phocas in the tenth century and the few sporadic similar later attempts, clearly failing to find currency and acceptance in the medieval Byzantine ideology of warfare.

Heraclius' anti-Persian wars and restitution of the True Cross inevitably played a role in crusading narratives and lore regarding Jerusalem and the Holy Land, as well as in the Western Christian legendary cycle and homilies related to the feast of the Exaltation of the Cross, including some eschatological conceptualizations of the conflict between Heraclius and Xusraw.[197] It was indeed the intense exploitation of eschatological notions in Heraclius' anti-Sasanian religious-military propaganda of the 620s (including those related to Jerusalem and the Holy Land) which came to exercise an enduring impact and enjoy a lasting *Nachleben* in Eastern Christendom as it predisposed the way in which the expansion of Muslim-

---

[196] Tyerman 2006:35.

[197] See the recent detailed survey of the Heraclius material in these cycles in Baert 2004:ch.3; on the related eschatological conceptualizations of the conflict between Heraclius and Chosroes, see Baert 2004:153-154.

Arab conquests in the Byzantine Levant and Egypt and the first signs of encroaching Islamization of the region were read and explained as events imbued with religious significance, triggering crucial phases in wider apocalyptic processes.[198] The consequent readjustments of apocalyptic schemes and periodization of eschatological history are evident in the principal works of East Christian (in general) and Byzantine (in particular) historico-eschatological apocalypticism which appeared in the second half of the seventh and eighth centuries, a period often seen as a formative one in the medieval Byzantine development of the genre.[199]

There are a number of indications that the seventh-century version of Syriac apocalyptic eschatology developed in the *Revelation of Pseudo-Methodius*, the *Eddesene Apocalypse* and *The Gospel of the Twelve Apostles* (which arose in response to expanding Islam) originally was conceived and gained influence in northern Mesopotamia and Syria, an area where the Christian communities were earlier in the century targeted by the religio-political propaganda of Heraclius' imperial government with its marked eschatologizing dimension. This cross-fertilization of seventh-century Byzantine imperial eschatology (as elaborated during the wars of the Heraclius' reign) and the distinctive Syriac apocalypticism which took shape in the course of the following decades of the century had a number of far-reaching implications. As the evidence of genuine Byzantine knowledge of Islam's religious doctrines does not predate the early eighth century, strong and lasting tendencies evolved which approached the religious and political Muslim-Arab challenge in the pre-conceived apocalyptic and eschatological patterns developed during the early seventh-century Sasanian-Byzantine wars and the attendant Jewish-Christian religious strife in the Holy Land and Jerusalem. The emergent Muslim-Arab power could thus be seen as heralding the eventual advent of the Antichrist (variously, within or outside the context of the Antichrist's perceived Jewish connection) and the establishment of the Caliphate as ushering in the end times era. Thus both Jews and Muslim Arabs could be identified as the main protagonists of the final conflicts of the last days in which they were to act as the principal political and religious adversaries of Christendom and the Christian empire in the events leading to the culmination of providential history, usually foreseen to take place in the Holy Land and Jerusalem.

---

198 See Kaegi 1969:146-147; Kaegi 1992:229-230; Whitby 1992:73-74; Cameron 1992:258-265; Olster 2006:54-55.

199 See Olster 1998:60; cf. Haldon 1990:367-68, and Magdalino 1993:30-32.

As later developments of these eschatological traditions were to become essential elements of the grand narrative of medieval Christian historical apocalypticism, it is thus indebted in a not inconsiderable manner to the Byzantine anti-Persian religio-political complex which took shape in response to the Sasanian conquest of Jerusalem in 614. It is to be hoped thus that by revisiting and reassessing the multifaceted evidence of some of the most dramatic episodes of the concluding stages of Sasanian-Byzantine interaction, while seeking to integrate into the analysis of the complex data on this subject material newly re-evaluated or made available, as well as examining the latest approaches and methodological considerations regarding its veracity and implications, this monograph has also contributed to the study of the afterlife and reverberations of this interaction in subsequent European and post-Sasanian Iranian contexts which clearly represent one of the most promising and under-explored fields in the religious and cultural histories of the medieval European and Iranian worlds.[200]

[200] See the recognition of this particular field of study as an area of a great potential for future research in Wiesehöfer 2006.

BIBLIOGRAPHY

Alexander 1967 = Alexander, Paul J.: *The Oracle of Baalbek: the Tiburtine Sibyl in Greek Dress*. (Dumbarton Oaks studies, 10). Washington, D.C.: Dumbarton Oaks Center for Byzantine Studies.

Alexander 1971 = Alexander, Paul J.: 'Byzantium and the Migration of Literary Works and Motifs: The Legend of the Last Roman Emperor'. *Medievalia et Humanistica*, n.s. 2, 1971, 47-68. Repr. in Alexander, Paul J.: *Religious and Political History and Thought in the Byzantine Empire*. XII. London: Variorum, 1978.

Alexander 1978 = Alexander, Paul J.: 'The Medieval Legend of the Last Roman Emperor and its Messianic Origin'. *Journal of the Warburg & Courtauld Institutes* 41, 1978, 1–15.

Alexander 1980 = Alexander, Paul J.: 'The Diffusion of Byzantine Apocalypses in the Medieval West and the Beginnings of Joachimism'. In: *Prophecy and Millenarianism: Essays in Honour of Marjorie Reeves*. Williams, Ann (ed.). Harlow: Longman. 55–106.

Alexander 1985 = Alexander, Paul J.: *The Byzantine Apocalyptic Tradition.* Abrahamse, Dorothy de F. (ed.). Berkeley, CA: University of California Press 1985.

Alexander 1977 = Alexander, Suzanne Spain: 'Heraclius, Byzantine Imperial Ideology and the David Plates'. *Speculum* 52, 1977, 217–237.

Altheim-Stiehl 1992 = Altheim-Stiehl, R.: 'The Sasanians in Egypt – Some Evidence of Historical Interest'. *Bulletin de la société d'archeologie copte* 31, 1992, 87–96.

Amit – Seligman – Zilberbod 2003 = Amit, D. – Seligman, J. – Zilberbod, I.: 'The 'Monastery of Theodoros and Cyriacus' on the Eastern Slope of Mount Scopus, Jerusalem.' In: Bottini – Di Segni – Chrupcala (eds.) 2003: 139–148.

Antiochus monachus, *Epistula* = Antiochus monachus: *Epistula ad Eustathium*, *Patrologia Graeca*, 89, cols.1421–1428.

Aphrahat, *Demonstration* 5 = 'Jacobi, episcopi Nisibeni, Homilia de adventu regis Persarum adversus urbem Nisibin'. Pereira, F. M. E. (ed.) In: *Orientalische Studien Theodor Nöldeke zum siebzigsten Geburtstag (2. März 1906) gewidmet von Freunden und Schülern und in ihrem Auftrag.* Bezold, Carl (ed.). Gieszen: A. Töpelmann 1906, vol. 2, 877–892

Arubas – Goldfus 2005 = Arubas, B – Goldfus, H. (eds.) *Excavations on the Site of the Jerusalem International Convention Center (Binyanei Ha`uma): A Settlement of the Late First to Second Temple Period, the Tenth Legion's Kilnworks, and a Byzantine Monastic Complex. The Pottery and Other Small Finds* (Journal of Roman Archaeology. Supplementary series, 1063–4304, No. 60). Porthsmouth RI: Journal of Roman Archaeology, 2005.

Athanassiadi 1981 = Athanassiadi, Polymnia: *Julian and Hellenism: an Intellectual Biography.* Oxford: Clarendon Press 1981.

Avi-Yonah 1949-50 = Avi-Yonah, Michael: 'Excavations at Sheikh Bader'. *Bulletin of the Jewish Palestine Exploration Society* 15,1949–1950, 19–24 (Hebrew).

Avi-Yonah 1984 = Avi-Yonah, Michael: *The Jews under Roman and Byzantine Rule. A Political History from the Bar Kokhba War to the Arab Conquest*. New York: Schocken Books; Jerusalem: Magnes, the Hebrew University 1984.

Avner 2003 = Avner, R.: 'The Recovery of the Kathisma Church and its Influence on Octagonal Buildings'. In: Bottini – Di Segni – Chrupcala (eds.) 2003: 73–86.

Avner 2006-2007 = Avner, R.: 'The Kathisma: a Christian and Muslim Pilgrimage Site'. *ARAM* 18–19, 2006–2007, 541–557.

Avni 2010 = Avni, Gideon: 'The Sack of Jerusalem by the Sassanian Persians (614) – an Archaeological Assessment'. *Bulletin of the American School of Oriental Research* 357, 2010, 35–48.

Avni – Baruch – Weksler-Bdolah 2001 = Avni, G. – Baruch, Y. – Weksler-Bdolah, S. 'Jerusalem, The Old City – Herod's Gate (A-2877)'. *Hadashot Arkheologiyot/Evacuations & Surveys in Israel* 113, 2001, 76–79.

Avni – Seligman 2003 = Avni, Gideon – Seligman, Jon: 'New Excavations at the Church of the Holy Sepulchre Compound'. In: Bottini – Di Segni – Chrupcala (eds.) 2003: 153–162.

Avni – Seligman (forthcoming) = Avni, Gideon – Seligman, Jon: 'Excavations at the Church of the Holy Sepulcher' *Atiqot*.

Bachrach 2003 = Bachrach, David S.: *Religion and the Conduct of War, c. 300-1215*. (Warfare in History). Woodbridge, Suffolk, UK: Boydell Press 2003.

Badilita 2005 = Badilita, Christian: *Métamorphoses de l'antichrist chez les pères de l'église*. (Théologie historique, 116). Paris: Beauchesne 2005.

Baert 2004 = Baert, Barbara: *A Heritage of Holy Wood: The Legend of the True Cross in Text and Image*. (Cultures, Beliefs and Traditions: Medieval and Early Modern Peoples, 22). Preedy. Lee (transl.). Leiden: Brill 2004.

Bahat 1999 = Bahat, Dan: 'The Golden Gate and the Date of the Madaba Map.' In: *The Madaba Map Centenary,1897–1997: Travelling through the Byzantine Umayyad Period:Proceedings of the International Conference Held in Amman, 7–9 April 1997*, (Studium Biblicum Franciscanum, Collectio Maior, 40). Piccirillo, Michele – Alliata, Eugenio (eds.). Jerusalem: Studium Biblicum Franciscanum 1999, 254–256.

Bainton 1946 = Bainton, Roland H.: 'The Early Church and War'. *Harvard Theological Review* 39, 1946, 189–213.

Bamberger 1940 = Bamberger, Bernard J.: 'A Messianic Document of the Seventh Century'. *Hebrew Union College Annual* 15, 1940, 425–431.

Bar 2003 = Bar, D: 'The Christianization of Rural Palestine during Late Antiquity'. *Journal of Ecclesiastical History* 54, 2003, 401–442.

Baras 1982 = Baras, Z. 'The Persian Conquest and the End of the Byzantine Rule'. In: *Eretz Israel from the Destruction of the Second Temple to the Muslim Conquest*. Baras, Z. – Safrai, S. – Tsafrir, Y. – Stern, M. (eds.). Jerusalem: Yad Ben Zvi 1982, 300–349. (Hebrew).

Baron 1957 = Baron, Salo W.: *A Social and Religious History of the Jews*, 2nd ed., vol. 3. New York: Columbia University Press 1957.

Barkay 1994 = Barkay, Gabriel: 'Excavations at Ketef Hinnom in Jerusalem'. In: *Ancient Jerusalem Revealed*, Geva. Hillel (ed.). Jerusalem: Israel Exploration Society 1994, 85–106.

Barnes 1981 = Barnes, Timothy David: *Constantine and Eusebius*. Cambridge, Mass. and London: Harvard University Press, 1981.

Barnes 1985 = Barnes, Timothy David: 'Constantine and the Christians of Persia'. *The Journal of Roman Studies* 75, 1985, 126–136.

Baynes 1904 = Baynes, Norman H.: 'The First Campaign of Heraclius against Persia'. *English Historical Review* 19, 1904, 694–702.

Baynes 1912 = Baynes, Norman H.: 'The Date of the Avar Surprise'. *Byzantinische Zeitschrift* 21, 1912, 110–128.

Baynes 1912a = Baynes, Norman H.: 'The Restoration of the Cross at Jerusalem'. *English Historical Review* 27, 1912, 287–299.

Baynes 1912-1913 = Baynes, Norman H.: 'The Military Operations of the Emperor Heraclius'. *United Service Magazine*. 46, 1912–13, 526–533, 659–666; 47, 1913, 30–38, 195–201, 318–324, 401–412, 532–541, 665–679.

Baynes 1951 = Baynes, Norman H.: 'The Icons before Iconoclasm'. *The Harvard Theological Review* 44, 1951, 98–106; repr. in: Baynes, Norman: *Byzantine Studies and Other Essays*. London: Athlone Press, 1955), XV, 226–239.

Ben-Dov 1975 = Ben-Dov, Meir: 'The Area South of the Temple Mount in the Early Islamic Period'. In: *Jerusalem Revealed: Archaeology in the Holy City, 1968-1974*, Yadin, Yigael – Stern, Ephraim (eds.); Grafman, R. (English transl. and abridgement). Jerusalem: Israel Exploration Society 1975, 97–101.

Ben-Dov 1982 = Ben-Dov, Meir, *In the Shadow of the Temple – The Discovery of Ancient Jerusalem*. Friedman, Ina (transl.). Jerusalem: Keter, 1982.

Berger 1985 = Berger, David: 'Three Typological Themes in Early Jewish Messianism: Messiah Son of Joseph, Rabbinic Calculations and the Figure of Armilus'. *Journal of the Association of Jewish Studies* 10, 1985, 141–164.

Bosworth 1999 = Bosworth, Clifford E. (transl.): *The History of al-Tabarī, Vol. V, The Sāsānids, the Byzantines, the Lakmids, and Yemen.* (SUNY series in Near Eastern studies. Bibliotheca Persica). Albany: State University of New York Press, 1999.

Bousset 1895 = Bousset, Wilhelm: *Der Antichrist in der Überlieferung des Judentums, des Neuen Testaments und der alten Kirche: ein Beitrag zur Auslegung der Apocalypse*. Göttingen: Vandenhoeck und Ruprecht.

Bottini – Di Segni – Chrupcala (eds.) 2003 = Bottini, G. C. – Di Segni, L. – Chrupcala, L. D. (eds.): *One Land, Many Cultures – Archaeological Studies in Honor of Stanislao Loffreda OFM.* (Studium Biblicum Franciscanum, Collectio Maior, 41). Jerusalem: Studium Biblicum Franciscanum 2003.

Bowersock 1978 = Bowersock, G.: *Julian the Apostate.* London: Duckworth , 1978.

Börm 2007 = Börm, Henning, *Prokop und die Perser: Untersuchungen zu den römisch-sasanidischen Kontakten in der ausgehenden Spätantike.* (Oriens et Occidens, 16). Stuttgart: Franz Steiner, 2007.

Brandes 1992 = Brandes, Wolfram: 'Heraclius between Restoration and Reform. Some Remarks on Recent Research'. In: Reinink – Stolte (eds.) 2002: 17–41.

Breydy 1981 = Breydy, M: 'Mamila ou Maqella? La prise de Jérusalem et ses conséquences (614 AD) selon la recension alexandrine des Annales d'Eutychès'. *Oriens Christianus* 65, 1981, 62–86.

Brock 1982 = Brock, Sebastian P.: 'Syriac Views of Emergent Islam'. In: *Studies on the First Century of Islamic Society.* (Papers on Islamic history, 5). Juynboll, G. H. A. (ed.). Carbondale, Ill.: Southern Illinois University Press 1982, 9–21. Repr. in: Brock, Sebastian P.: *Syriac Perspectives on Late Antiquity*, VIII. London: Variorum, 1984.

Brock 1982a = Brock, Sebastian P.: 'Christians in the Sasanian Empire. A Case of Divided Loyalties'. In: *Religion and National Identity: Papers Read at the Nineteenth Summer Meeting and the Twentieth Winter Meeting of the Ecclesiastical History Society.* (Studies in Church History, 18). Mews, Stewart (ed.). Oxford: Published for the Ecclesiastical History Society by B. Blackwell, 1982, 1–19.

Cadoux 1919 = Cadoux, Cecil, John: *The Early Christian Attitude to War.* London: Headley 1919.

Cameron 1969 = Cameron, Averil: 'Agathias on the Sasanians'. *Dumbarton Oaks Papers* 23, 1969, 67–183.

Cameron 1979 = Cameron, Averil: 'The Virgin's Robe: An Episode in the History of Early Seventh-Century Constantinople'. *Byzantion.* 49, 1979, 42–56. Repr. in: Cameron 1981, XVII.

Cameron 1981 = Cameron, Averil: *Continuity and Change in Sixth-Century Byzantium.* London: Variorum 1981.

Cameron 1991 = Cameron, Averil: 'Disputations, Polemical Literature and the Formation of Opinion in the Early Byzantine Period'. In: *Dispute Poems and Dialogues in the Ancient and Mediaeval Near East: Forms and Types of Literary Debates in Semitic and Related Literatures* (Orientalialovaniensia analecta, 42), Reinink, Gerrit J. – Vanstiphout, H. L. J. (eds.). Leuven: Peeters 1991, 91–108.

Cameron 1991a = Cameron, Averil: 'The Eastern Provinces in the Seventh Century A. D. Hellenism and the Emergence of Islam'. In: *Hellenismos: Quelques jalons pour une histoire de l'identité greque* (Travaux du Centre de recherche sur le Proche-Orient et la Grèce antiques, 11), Said, Suzanne (ed.). Leiden; New York: Brill, 287–313. Repr. in: Cameron 1981, IV.

Cameron 1992 = Cameron, Averil: 'Byzantium and the Past in the Seventh Century: the Search for Redefinition'. In: *Le septième siècle: changements et continuités/The Seventh Century: Change and Continuity.* (Studies of the Warburg Institute, 42). Fontaine Jacques – Hillgarth, Jocelyn N. (eds.). London: Warburg Institute, University of London 1992, 250–276.

Cameron 1994 = Cameron, Averil: 'The Jews in Seventh-Century Palestine'. *Scripta Classica Israelica* 13, 1994, 75–93.

Cameron 1995 = Cameron, Averil: 'The "Trophies of Damascus": the Church, the Temple and Sacred Space. In: *Temple, Lieu de Conflit (Les cahiers du CEPOA, Actes du colloque de Cartigny 1988)*. Louvain: Peeters 1995, 203–212.

Cameron 1996 = Cameron, Averil: 'Byzantines and Jews: Some Recent Works on Early Byzantium'. *Byzantine and Modern Greek Studies* 20, 1996, 249–274.

Cameron 2002 = Cameron, Averil: 'Blaming the Jews: the Seventh-Century Invasions of Palestine in Context'. *Melange Gilbert Dagron, Travaux et Mémoires* 14, 2002, 57–78.

Carile 1994 = Carile, Antonio: *Materiali di storia bizantina,* Bologna: Lo Scarabeo 1994.

Carile 2000 = Carile, Antonio: 'Political Interaction between Byzantium and Iran in VIIth Century'. In: *Kontakte zwischen Iran, Byzanz und der Steppe im 6.–7. Jh.* (Varia Archaeologica Hungarica, 9). Bálint, Csanád (ed.). Budapest, Naples & Rome: Akadémiai kiadó 2000, 137–144.

Carile 2005 = Carile, Antonio, 'La guerra santa nella Romània (impero romano d'Oriente) secoli VII-XI.' In: *Guerra santa, guerra e pace dal Vicino Oriente antico alle tradizioni ebraica, cristiana e islamica.* Perani, M. (ed.). Florence: Giuntina, 2005, 251–261.

Casey 1989 = Casey, M.: 'The Fourth Kingdom in Cosmas Indicopleustes and the Syrian Tradition'. *Rivista di Storia e Letteratura Religiosa* 25, 1989, 385–403.

Cerulli 1946 = Cerulli, E. 'La "Conquista persiana di Gerusalemme" ed altre fonti orientali cristiane di un episodio dell' "Orlando Furioso"'. *Orientalia* 15, 1946, 439–481.

Chaumont 1988 = Chaumont, M. L.: *La Christianisation de l'empire iranien des origins aux grandes persecutions du IVe siècle.* (Corpus scriptorum Christianorum Orientalium, 499; Subsidia, 80). Louven: Peeters 1988.

Christensen 1936 = Christensen, Arthur: *L'Iran sous les Sassanides.* (Annales du Musée Guimet. Bibliothèque d'études, 48). Copenhagen: Levin & Munksgaard; Paris: P. Geuthner 1936.

Chronicon paschale = *Chronicon paschale* (Corpus scriptorum historiae Byzantinae, 7-8). Dindorf, Ludwig (ed.). 2 vols., Bonn: Weber 1832. Partial English translation: *Chronicon Paschale 284–628 AD.* (Translated texts for historians, 7). Whitby, Michael – Whitby, Mary (transl.). Liverpool: Liverpool University Press 1989.

Clermont-Ganneau 1898 = Clermont-Ganneau, C.: 'The Taking of Jerusalem by the Persians, A.D. 614'. *Palestine Exploration Fund Quarterly Statement* 1898, 38–54.

Conybeare 1910 = Conybeare, Frederick C.: 'Antiochus Strategos' Account of the Sack of Jerusalem in A.D. 614'. *The English Historical Review* 25, 1910, 502–517.

Couret 1897 = Couret, Alphonse: 'La Prise de Jerusalem par le Perses en 614'. *Revue de l'Orient Chrétien* 2, 1897, 125–164.

Creswell 1969 = Creswell, Keppel A. C.: *Early Muslim Architecture, Vol. 1, Umayyads A.D. 622-750.* 2 vols. Oxford: Clarendon Press 1969.

Crowfoot – Fitzgerald 1929 = Crowfoot, J. W. – Fitzgerald, G. M.: *Excavations in the Tyropoeon Valley, Jerusalem, 1927.* (Annual of the Palestine Exploration Fund 5). London: Palestine Exploration Fund 1929.

Dagron 1974 = Dagron, Gilbert: *Naissance d'une capitale: Constantinople et ses institutions de 330 à 451.* (Bibliothèque byzantine. Etudes, 7). Paris: Preses universitaires de France 1974.

Dagron 1991 = Dagron, Gilbert: 'Introduction historique'. In: Dagron – Déroche 1991: 17–46.

Dagron 1991a = Dagron, Gilbert: 'Judaïser'. *Travaux et Mémoires* 11, 1991, 359–380.

Dagron 1997 = Dagron, Gilbert: 'Byzance entre le djihad et la croisade: quelque remarques.' In: *Le concile de Clermont de 1095 et l'appel à la Croisade: actes du Colloque universitaire international de Clermont-Ferrand (23-25 juin 1995)/organisé et publié avec le concours du Conseil régional d'Auvergne.* (Collection de l'École française de Rome, 236). Rome: Ecole française de Rome, Palais Farnèse 1997, 325–327.

Dagron 2003 = Dagron, Gilbert: *Emperor and Priest. The Imperial Office in Byzantium.* (Past and present publications). Birrell. J (transl.). Cambridge: Cambridge University Press 2003.

Dagron – Déroche 1991 = Dagron, Gilbert – Déroche, Vincent: 'Juifs et Chrétiens dans l'Orient du VIIe siècle'. *Travaux et Mémoires* 11, 1991, 17–273.

Daley 1991 = Daley, Brian E.: *The Hope of the Early Church: A Handbook of Patristic Eschatology.* Cambridge: Cambridge University Press 1991.

Daley 2008 = Daley, Brian E: 'Eschatology in the Early Church Fathers'. In: *The Oxford Handbook of Eschatology.* (Oxford handbooks). Walls, J. L. (ed.), New York; Oxford: Oxford University Press 2008, 91–109.

Dan 1998 = Dan, Joseph: 'Armilus: The Jewish Antichrist and the Origin and Dating of Sefer Zerubbabel'. In: *Toward the Millennium. Messianic Expectations from the Bible to Waco.* (Studies in the history of religions, 77). Schäfer, Peter – Cohen, Mark (eds.). Leiden: Brill 1998, 73–105.

Daryaee 1997 = Daryaee, Touraj: 'Religio-Political Propaganda on the Coins of Xusrō II'. *American Journal of Numismatics* 7, 1997, 141–154.

Dauphin 1998 = Claudine, Dauphin: *La Palestine byzantine. Peuplement et populations.* (BAR international series, 726). 3 vols., Oxford: Archaeopress 1998.

Decret 1979 = Decret, F.: 'Les consequences sur le christianisme en Perse de l'affrontement des empires romain et sassanide. De Shapur Ie à Yazdgard Ie'. *Recherche augustiniennes* 14, 1979, 91–152.

De Lange 1978 = De Lange, Nicholas R. M.: 'Jewish Attitudes to the Roman Empire'. In: *Imperialism in the Ancient World* (Cambridge classical studies), Garnsey, Peter D. A – Whittaker, Charles R. (eds.). Cambridge: Cambridge University Press 1978, 255–281.

De Lange 1992 = De Lange, Nicholas R. M: 'Jews and Christians in the Byzantine Empire: problems and prospects'. In: *Christianity and Judaism: papers read at the 1991 Summer Meeting and the 1992 Winter Meeting of the Ecclesiastical History Society*. (Studies in church history, 29). Wood, Diana (ed.). Oxford: Blackwell 1992, 15–32.

De Lange 2005 = De Lange, Nicholas R. M: 'Jews in the Age of Justinian'. In: *The Cambridge Companion to the Age of Justinian*, Mcihael Maas, Michael (ed.). Cambridge: Cambridge University Press 2005, 401–427.

Delehaye 1909 = Delehaye, Hippolyte: *Les légendes grecques des saints militaries*, Paris: Librairie A. Picard 1909.

Delehaye 1927 = Delehaye, Hippolyte (ed.): 'Une Vie inédite de Saint Jean l'Aumonier'. *Analecta Bollandiana* 45, 1927, 5–74.

Dennis 1984 = Dennis, George T. (transl.): *Maurice's Strategikon: Handbook of Byzantine Military Strategy.* (The Middle Ages). Philadelphia: University of Pennsylvania Press, 1984.

Dennis 1985 = Dennis, George T. (ed. and transl.): *Three Byzantine Military Treatises.* (Dumbarton Oaks texts, 9; Corpus fontium historiae Byzantinae, 25; Series Washingtonensis). Washington D. C.: Dumbarton Oaks, Research Library and Collection 1985.

Dennis 1993 = Dennis, George T.: 'Religious Services in the Byzantine Army'. In: *Eulogēma: Studies in Honor of Robert Taft, S.J.* (Studia Anselmiana, 110; Analecta liturgica, 17). Carr, E. et al. (eds.). Rome: Pontificio Ateneo S. Anselmo 1993, 107–118.

Dennis 2001 = Dennis, George T.: 'Defenders of the Christian People: Holy War in Byzantium'. In: *The Crusades from the Perspective of Byzantium and the Muslim World*, Laiou, Angeliki E. – Mottaheden, Roy Parviz (eds.). Washington, D.C.: Dumbarton Oaks, Research Library and Collection 2001, 31–41.

deSilva 1996 = deSilva, David, 'The Revelation to John: A Case Study in Apocalyptic Propaganda and the Maintenance of Sectarian Identity'. *Sociological Analysis* 53(4), 1996, 375–395.

Devréesse 1937 = Devréesse, Robert (ed.): 'La fin inedited d'une letter de S. Maxime: un baptême force de Juifs et Samaritains á Carthage en 632'. *Revue des sciences religieuses* 17, 1937, 25–35.

Dignas - Winter 2007 = Dignas, Beate – Winter, Engelbert: *Rome and Persia in Late Antiquity: Neighbours and Rivals*, Cambridge, UK & New York: Cambridge University Press, 2007.

Doctrina Jacobi nuper baptizati = *Doctrina Jacobi nuper baptizati*, Déroche, Vincente (ed.). In: Dagron – Déroche, 1991: 47–229.

Drijvers 2002 = Drijvers, Jan W.: 'Heraclius and the *Restitutio Crucis*: Notes on Symbolism and Ideology'. In: Reinink – Stolte (eds.) 2002: 175–191.

Drijvers 2006 = Drijvers, Jan W.: 'Ammianus Marcellinus' Image of Sasanian Society'. In: Huyse, Philip – Wiesehöfer, Josef (eds.): *Ērān ud Anērān: Studien zu den Beziehungen zwischen dem Sasanidenreich und der Mittelmeerwelt. Beiträge des Internationalen Colloquiums in Eutin, 8.–9. Juni 2000* (Oriens et Occidens, 13), Stuttgart: Steiner 2006, 45–71.

Drijvers – Hunt (eds.) 1999 = Drijvers, Jan W. – Hunt, David (eds.). *The Late Roman World and Its Historian: Interpreting Ammianus Marcellinus*. London: Routledge 1999.

Edelstein – Dauphine 1975 = Edelstein, G. Dauphine, C.: 'A Byzantine Church at Nahariya'. *Qadmoniot* 8, 1975, 128–132 (Hebrew).

Ekkebus 2009 = Ekkebus, Bob: 'Heraclius and the Evolution of Byzantine Strategy'. *Constructing the Past* 10:1, 2009, Article 11, 72–96. Available at: http://digitalcommons.iwu.edu/constructing/vol10/iss1/1; seen on 10.05.2011).

Eutychius, *Annales* = Breydy, Michael (ed.). *Das Annalenwerk des Eutychius von Alexandrien: Ausgewähle Geschichten und Legenden kompiliert von Sa'id ibn Batrīk um 935 A.D.* (Corpus scriptorum Christianorum Orientalium, 471–472; Scriptores Arabici, 44–45), 2 vols., Louvain: Peeters 1985.

Farrokh = Farrokh, Kaveh: *Shadows in the Desert: Ancient Persia at War.* Oxford: Osprey 2007.

Field 1999 = Field, Lester L.: *Liberty, Dominion, and the Two Swords: On the Origins of Western Political Theology (180–398).* (Publications in medieval studies, 18). Notre Dame, Ind.: University of Notre Dame Press, 1998.

Fleischer 1971 = Fleischer, Ezra: 'An Ancient Jewish Tradition on the Date of the End of Byzantine Rule in Eretz Israel'. *Zion* 36, 1971, 110–115 (Hebrew).

Fleischer 1984-85 = Fleischer, Ezra: 'Solving the Qilliri Riddle'. *Tarbiz* 54, 1984–1985, 383–427 (Hebrew).

Flusin 1992 = Flusin, Bernard: *Saint Anastase le Perse et l'histoire de la Palestine au début du VIIe siècle.* (Le monde byzantin). 2 vols. Paris: Ed. du C.N.R.S. 1992.

Foss 1975 = Foss, Clive: 'The Persians in Asia Minor and the End of Antiquity'. *The English Historical Review.* 90 (357), 1975, 721–747.

Foss 2003 = Foss, Clive: 'The Persians in the Roman Near East (602-630 AD)'. *Journal of the Royal Asiatic Society* 3, 13, 2, 2003, 149–170.

Fowden 1993 = Fowden, Garth: *Empire to Commonwealth: Consequences of Monotheism in Late Antiquity*. Princeton, N.J.: Princeton University Press 1993.

Fowden 1994 = Fowden, Garth: 'The Last Days of Constantine: Oppositional Versions and Their Influence'. *The Journal of Roman Studies*, 84, 1994, 146–170.

Fowden 1999 = Fowden, Elizabeth K.: *The Barbarian Plain: Saint Sergius between Rome and Iran.* (The Transformation of the Classical Heritage, 28). Berkeley; Los Angeles: University of California Press 1999

Fredriksen – Irshai 2006 = Fredriksen, P. – Irshai, O.: 'Christian Anti Judaism: Polemics and Politics'. In: *The Cambridge History of Judaism*, vol. 4, *The Late Roman-Rabbinic Period.* Katz, S. T. (ed.). Cambridge: Cambridge University Press 2006, 977–1034.

Frendo 1992 = Frendo, David: 'Sassanian Irredentism and the Foundation of Constantinople: Historical Truth and Historical Reality'. *Bulletin of the Asia Institute*, n.s. 6, 1992, 59–68.

Frendo 1995 = Frendo, David: 'The Early Exploits and Final Overthrow of Khusrau II (591–628): Panegyric and Vilification in the Last Byzantine-Iranian Conflict'. *Bulletin of the Asia Institute*, n.s. 9, 1995, 209–214.

Frendo 1997 = Frendo, David: 'The Religious Factor in Byzantine-Iranian Relations'. *Bulletin of the Asia Institute*, n.s. 11, 1997, 105–123.

Frendo 2000 = Frendo, David: 'Byzantine-Iranian Relations Before and After the Death of Khusrau II: A Critical Examination of the Evidence'. *Bulletin of the Asia Institute,* n. s., 14, 2000, 27–45.

Frendo 2001 = Frendo, David: 'Constantine's Letter to Shapur II, Its Authenticity, Occasion, and Attendant Circumstances'. *Bulletin of the Asia Institute* 15, 2001, 57–71.

Frendo 1986 = Frendo, J. D. C.: 'Classical and Christian Influences in the *Heracliad* of George of Pisidia'. *Classical Bulletin* 62, 1986, 53–62.

Freshfield 1947 = Freshfield, Edwin Hanson (ed. and transl.): *Roman Law in the Later Roman Empire. Military Discipline of the Emperor Maurice, c. A.D. 590, from the Strategikon*, Cambridge: Cambridge University Press 1947.

Frolow 1953 = Frolow, Anatole: 'La vraie Croix et les expéditions d'Héraclius en Perse'. *Revue des études byzantines* 11, 1953, 88–105.

Gariboldi 2009 = Gariboldi, Andrea: 'Social Conditions in Egypt under the Sasanian Occupation'. *La Parola del Passato* 64, 2009, 321–353.

Garsoïan 1973 = Garsoïan, Nina: 'Le rôle de la hiérarchie chrétienne dans les rapports diplomatiques entre Byzance et les Sassanides'. *Revue des Etudes Arméniennes* n.s. 10, 1973, 119–138.

George of Pisidia, *Expeditio Persica* = *Expeditio Persica.* In: *Giorgio di Pisidia, Poemi. I. Panegirici Epici*, (Studia patristica et Byzantina; 7). Pertusi, Agostino (ed. and transl.). Ettal: Buch-Kunstverlag 1959, 84–136; *Expeditio Persica.* In: *Carmi. Giorgio di Pisidia.* (Classici greci). Tartaglia, Luigi (ed. and transl.). Torino: Unione tipografico-editrice torinese 1998, 71–141.

Gerland 1894 = Gerland, E.: 'Die persischen Feldzüge des Kaisers Herakleios'. *Byzantinische Zeitschrift* 3, 1894, 330–373.

Geva 1992 = Geva, H.: 'Jerusalem, the Byzantine Period'. In: *New Encyclopedia of Archaeological Excavations in the Holy Land,* vol. 2., Stern, E. – Gilboa, A. (eds.). Jerusalem: Israel Exploration Society 1992, 768–785.

Gil 1996 = Gil, Moshe: 'The Political History of Jerusalem during the early Muslim Period'. In: *The History of Jerusalem: the Early Muslim Period, 638-1099.* Prawer, Joshua – Ben-Shammai, Haggai (eds.). Jerusalem: Yad Izhak Ben-Zvi; New York: New York University Press 1996, 1–37.

Gnoli 1989 = Gnoli, Gherardo: *The Idea of Iran: an Essay on its Origin* (Serie orientale Roma, 62). Rome: Istituto italiano per il Medio ed Estremo Oriente & Leiden: Brill 1989.

Graham 2009 = Graham Susan L.: 'Justinian and the Politics of Space'. In: *Constructions of Space II: The Biblical City and Other Imagined Spaces.* (Library of Hebrew Bible / Old Testament studies, 490). Berquist, J. L. – Camp, C. V. (eds.). New York; London: T. &T. Clark 2009, 53–78.

Grant 1980 = Grant, Robert M.: 'War – Just, Holy, Unjust – in Hellentistic and Early Christian Thought'. *Augustinianum* 20, 1980, 173–189.

Greatrex 2003 = Greatrex, Geoffrey: 'Khusro II and the Christians of His Empire'. *Journal of the Canadian Society for Syriac Studies* 3, 2003, 78–88.

Greatrex – Lieu 2002 = Greatrex, Geoffrey – Lieu, Samuel N. C. (eds.): *The Roman Eastern Frontier and the Persian Wars. Part II, AD 36–630. A Narrative Sourcebook.* London: Routledge 2002.

Groh 1985 = Groh, D. I.: 'The Onomastikon of Eusebius and the Rise of Christian Palestine'. *Studia Patristica* 18, 1985, 23–32.

Grousset 1934 = Grousset, René: *Histoire des croisades et du royaume fran de Jérusalem*, Paris: Plon 1934.

Gruen 2005 = Gruen, Erich S. (ed.): *Cultural Borrowings and Ethnic Appropriations in Antiquity*. (Oriens et Occidens, 8). Stuttgart: Steiner 2005.

Guidi 1903 = Guidi, I. (ed. and tr.) *Chronicon anonymum.* In: Guidi, I. (ed. and tr.) *Chronica minora I.* (Corpus scriptorum Christianorum orientalium. 1, 2. Scriptores Syri, 1, 2). Louvain 1903.

Guillaumont 1969-70 = Guillaumont, A.: 'Justinien et l'église de Perse'. *Dumbarton Oaks Papers* 23–24, 1969–1970, 41–66.

Guran 2006 = Guran, Petre: 'Genesis and Function of the Last Emperor-Myth in Byzantium'. *Bizantinistica. Rivista di Studi Bizantini e Slavi*, 2ª serie, 8, 2006, 273–303.

Haldon 1990 = Haldon, John: *Byzantium in the Seventh Century: the Transformation of a Culture*. Cambridge: Cambridge University Press. 1990 (2nd rev. ed., 1997).

Haldon 1999 = Haldon, John: *Warfare, State and Society in the Byzantine World, 565-1204.* (Warfare and History). London: University College Press 1999.

Haldon 2007 = Haldon, John (ed.): *Byzantine Warfare.* (International library of essays on military history). Aldershot: Ashgate, 2007.

Harakas 1981 = Harakas, Stanley S.: 'The Morality of War'. In: *Orthodox Synthesis. The Unity of Theological Thought*, Allen, Joseph J. (ed.). Crestwood, New York: St Vladimir Seminar Press 1981, 67–95.

Harakas 1999 = Harakas, Stanley S.: *The Wholeness of Faith and Life: Orthodox Christian Ethics: Part One. Patristic Ethics*, Brookline, MA: Holy Orthodox Press 1999.

Harnack 1905 = Harnack, Adolf von: *Militia Christi: Die christliche Religion und der Soldatenstand in der ersten drei Jahrhunderten.* Tübingen: Mohr/Siebeck 1905.

Heid 1993 = Heid, Stefan: *Chiliasmus und Antichrist-Mythos: eine frühchristliche Kontroverse um das Heilige Land* (Hereditas 6). Bonn: Borengässer 1993.

Hill 1992 = Hill, Charles E: *Regnum Caelorum: Patterns of Future Hope in Early Christianity*. (Oxford Early Christian Studies). Oxford: Clarendon 1992.

Himmelfarb 1990 = Himmelfarb, Marta: 'Sefer Zerubbabel'. In: *Rabbinic Fantasies. Imaginative Narratives from Classical Hebrew Literature*, Stern,

David – Mirsky, Mark J. (eds.). Philadelphia: Jewish Publication Society, 1990, 69–90.

Himmelfarb 2002 = Himmelfarb, Marta: 'The Mother of the Messiah in the Talmud Yerushalmi and Sefer Zerubbabel'. In: *The Talmud Yerushalmi and Graeco-Roman Culture.* (Texte und Studien zum antiken Judentum, 93). Schäfer, Peter (ed.). Tübingen: Mohr/Siebeck 2002, 369–390.

Hirschfeld 1992 = Hirschfeld, Y.: *The Judean Desert Monasteries in the Byzantine Period.* New Haven: Yale University Press 1992.

The History of Lazar P'arpets'i = *The History of Lazar P'arpets'i.* (Suren D. Fesjian academic publications, 4). Thomson, Robert W. (transl.). Atlanta, Ga.: Scholars Press 1991.

Holdenried 2004 = Holdenried, Anke: *The Sibyl and her Scribes: Manuscripts and Interpretation of the Latin Sibylla Tiburtina c. 1050-1500.* (Church, faith, and culture in the Medieval West). Aldershot: Ashgate, 2004.

Holum 1977 = Holum, Kenneth G., 'Pulcheria's Crusade A.D. 421–22 and the Ideology of Imperial Victory'. *Greek, Roman and Byzantine Studies* 18:2, 1977, 153–172.

Holum – Hohlfelder – Vann – Maltese 1988 = Holum, Kenneth G. –Hohlfelder, Robert L. – Vann, Robert L. – Maltese, Roberta Blender (eds.), *King Herod's Dream: Caesarea on the Sea.* New York & London: Norton 1988.

House 1888 = House, C. (ed. and transl.): 'Vita sancti Georgii Chozibitae auctore Anonio Chozibita'. *Analecta Bollandiana* 7, 1888, 95–144, 336–359.

Howard-Johnston 1994 = Howard-Johnston, James: 'The Official History of Heraclius' Persian Campaigns.' In: *The Roman and Byzantine Army in the East*, Dąbrowa, E. (ed.). Kraków: Uniwersytet Jagielloński, Instytut Historii 1994, 57–87. Repr. in: Howard-Johnston 2006a, IV.

Howard-Johnston 1995 = Howard-Johnston, James: 'The Siege of Constantinople in 626'. In: *Constantinople and its Hinterland: Papers from the Twenty-seventh Spring Symposium of Byzantine Studies, Oxford, April 1993,* (Publications/Society for the Promotion of Byzantine Studies, 3). Mango, Cyril – Dagron, Gilbert – Greatrex, Geoffrey (eds.). Aldershot, UK; Brookfield, Vt., USA: Variorum 1995, 131–142. Repr. in: Howard-Johnston 2006a, VII.

Howard-Johnston 1996 = Howard-Johnston, James: 'Heraclius' Persian Campaign and the Revival of the East Roman Empire'. *War in History* 6, 1996, 1–44. Repr. in: Howard-Johnston 2006a, VIII.

Howard-Johnston 2002 = Howard-Johnston, James: 'Armenian Historians of Heraclius. An Examination of the Aims, Sources and Working-Methods of Sebeos and Movses Daskhurantsi'. In: Reinink – Stolte (eds.) 2002: 41–62. Repr. in: Howard-Johnston 2006a, V.

Howard-Johnston 2004 = Howard-Johnston, James: 'Pride and Fall: Khusro II and His Regime, 626–628'. In: *Atti del Convegno internazionale sul tema La Persia e Bisanzio. Accademia Nazionale dei Lincei, Roma, 14–18 ottobre 2002.* (Atti dei Convegni Lincei 201), Gnoli, Gherardo (ed.). Rome: Accademia Nazionale dei Lincei 2004, 93–113. Repr. in: Howard-Johnston 2006a, IX.

Howard-Johnston 2006 = Howard-Johnston, James: 'Al-Tabari on the Last Great War of Antiquity'. In: Howard-Johnston 2006a, 1–22.

Howard-Johnston 2006a = Howard-Johnston, James: *East Rome, Sasanid Persia and the End of Antiquity*. (Variorum collected studies series). Aldershot: Ashgate, 2006.

Howard-Johnston 2010 = Howard-Johnston, James, *Witnesses to a World Crisis: Historians and Histories of the Middle East in the Seventh Century*, Oxford: Oxford University Press, 2010.

Horowitz 1998 = Horowitz, Elliott: '"The Vengeance of the Jews Was Stronger than Their Avarice": Modern Historians and the Persian Conquest of Jerusalem in 614'. *Jewish Social Studies* 4, 1998, 1–39.

Hoyland 1997 = Hoyland, Robert G.: *Seeing Islam as Others Saw It: a Survey and Evaluation of Christian, Jewish, and Zoroastrian Writings on Early Islam.* (Studies in late antiquity and early Islam, 13) Princeton, N.J.: Darwin Press 1997.

Huber 2008 = Huber, Irene: 'Ansichten eines Zivilisierten über die unzivilisierte Welt: Das Sāsāniden-Bild des Georgios Pisides und sein historischer Wert für den spätantiken Iran'. *Klio* 90/1, 2008, 162–192.

Hunt 1982 = Hunt, E. D.: Holy Land Pilgrimage in the Later Roman Empire, AD 312–460. Oxford: Clarendon Press; New York: Oxford University Press 1982.

Huyse 2002 = Huyse, Philip, 'La revendication de territoires achéménides par les Sassanides: une réalité historique?' In: *Iran. Questions et connaissances. Actes du IVe Congrès européen des études iraniennes, organisé par la Societas Iranologica Europaea, Paris, 6–10 septembre 1999*, vol. I: *La période ancienne.* Huyse, Philip (ed.). (Cahiers de Studia Iranica 25). Paris; Louvain: Peeters / AAEI, 297–311.

Huyse – Wiesehöfer (eds.) 2006 = Huyse, Philip – Wiesehöfer, Josef (eds.) *Ērān ud Anērān: Studien zu den Beziehungen zwischen dem Sasanidenreich und der Mittelmeerwelt; Beiträge des Internationalen Colloquiums in Eutin, 8.–9. Juni 2000* (Oriens et Occidens, 13), Stuttgart: Steiner, 2006.

Impellizzeri 1985 = Impellizzeri, Salvatore: 'Aux racines de l'idée de croisade et sa survie dans les idéologies politiques'. *Nicolaus* 12/2, 1985, 339–348.

Ioannis Skylitzes, *Synopsis* = Ioannis Skylitzes, *Synopsis Historiarum.* (Corpus fontium historiae Byzantinae 5). Thurn, Hans (ed.). New York; Berlin: de Gruyter 1973.

Irshai 1999 = Irshai, O.: 'The Jerusalem Bishopric and the Jews in the Fourth Century: History and Eschatology'. In: Levine (ed.) 1999, 204–221.

Jacoby – Tsafrir 1988 = Jacoby, D. – Tsafrir, Y. (eds.): *Jews, Samaritans and Christians in Byzantine Palestine.* Jerusalem: Yad Ben- Zvi 1988 (Hebrew).

Jacobs 2004 = Jacobs, Andrew: *Remains of the Jews: the Holy Land and Christian Empire in Late Antiquity.* Stanford: Stanford University Press, 2004.

Join-Lambert 1958 = Join-Lambert, Michel: *Jerusalem.* Haldane, Charlotte (trans.), London: Elek Books; New York: Putnam, 1958.

Kaegi 1969 = Kaegi, Walter Emil: 'Initial Byzantine Reactions to the Arab Conquest.' *Church History* 38/2, 1969, 139–149.

Kaegi 1992 = Kaegi, Walter Emil: *Byzantium and the Early Islamic Conquests*. Cambridge: Cambridge University Press 1992.

Kaegi 2003 = Kaegi, Walter Emil: *Heraclius, Emperor of Byzantium*. Cambridge, UK and New York: Cambridge University Press 2003.

Kaplony 2002 = Kaplony, Andreas: *The Haram of Jerusalem 324–1099. Temple, Friday Mosque, Area of Spiritual Power.* (Freiburger Islamstudien, 22). Stuttgart: Steiner 2002.

Kloner 2003 = Kloner, A.: *Archaeological Survey of Israel, Survey of Jerusalem – The Northwestern Sector, Introduction and Indices,* Jerusalem: Israel Antiquities Authority 2003.

Kolbaba 1998 = Kolbaba, Tia M.: 'Fighting for Christianity: Holy War in the Byzantine Empire'. *Byzantion* 68, 1998, 194–221.

Kolia-Dermitzakē 1991 = Kolia-Dermitzakē, Athēna: *Ho byzantinos "hieros polemos": hē ennoia kai hē provolē tou thrēskeutikou polemou sto Byzantio.* (Historikes monographies, 10). Athens: Historikes Ekdoseis St. D. Basilopoulos.

Kondakov 1904 = Kondakov, Nikodim P.: *Arkheologicheskoe puteshestvie po Sirii i Palestine*. St Petersburg, 1904.

Krauss 1902 = Krauss, Samuel: 'Der römisch-persische Krieg in der jüdischen Elia Apokalypse'. *Jewish Quarterly Review* 14, 1902, 359– 372.

Krauss 1996 = Krauss, Samuel: *The Jewish-Christian Controversy from the Earliest Times to 1789*. (Texte und Studien zum antiken Judentum, 56). Horbury, William (ed. and rev.). Tübingen: Mohr/Siebeck 1996.

Labourt 1904 = Labourt, J.: *Le Christianisme dans l'empire perse sous la dynastie sassanide.* Paris 1904.

Laga 1990 = Laga, Carl: 'Judaism and Jews in Maximus Confessor's Works. Theoretical Controversy and Practical Attitude'. *Byzantinoslavica* 51, 1990, 177–188.

Laiou 1993 = Laiou, Angeliki E.: 'On Just War in Byzantium'. In *To Hellenikon: Vol. 1, Hellenic Antiquity and Byzantium. Studies in Honor of Speros Vryonis Jr*, Langdon, J. et al. (eds.), New Rochelle, N.Y.: Aristide D. Caratzas 1993, 153–177.

Laiou 2006 = Laiou, Angeliki E.: 'The Just War of Eastern Christians and the Holy War of the Crusaders'. In: *The Ethics of War: Shared Problems in Different Traditions*. Sorabji, Richard – Rodin, David (eds.). Aldershot, Hants: Ashgate 2006, 30–44.

Laurent 1946 = Laurent, Vitalien: 'L'idée de guerre sainte et la tradition byzantine'. *Revue historique du sud-est européen* 23, 1946, 71–98.

Leder 1987 = Leder, Stefan: 'The Attitude of the Population, especially the Jews, towards the Arab-Islamic Conquest of Bilād al Shām and the Question of Their Role Therein'. *Die Welt des Orients* 18, 1987, 64–71.

Lemerle 1955 = Lemerle, Paul: 'Byzance et la croisade'. In: *Relazioni del X Congresso internazionale di scienze storiche, Roma, 4-11 settembre 1955.* (Biblioteca storica Sansoni, n.s. 22). Firenze: G. C. Sansoni 1955, 595–620.

Lemerle 1955 = Lemerle, Paul: 'Quelques remarques sur le regne d'Heraclius'. *Studi medievali*, 3rd ser., 1, 1960, 347–361.

Leonis Imperatoris tactica = *Leonis Imperatoris tactica.* (Sylloge tacticorum Graecorum, 3). Vári, Rezsö (ed.). Budapest: Typis Regiae universitatis scientiarum budapestinensis, 2 vols., 1917–1922.

Lévi 1914 = Lévi, Israël: 'Une apocalypse judéo-arabe'. *Revue des études juives* 67, 1914, 178–182.

Lévi 1914a = Lévi, Israël: 'L'Apocalypse de Zorobabel et le roi de Perse Siroès'. *Revue des études juives* 68, 1914, 129–160; 69, 1914, 108–121.

Lévi 1994 = Lévi, Israël: *La ravissement du Messie à sa naissance et autres essays.* Paris; Louvain: Peeters 1994.

Levine (ed.) 1999 = Levine, Lee I. (ed.): *Jerusalem: Its Sanctity and Centrality to Judaism, Christianity and Islam.* New York: Continuum 1999.

Lewis 1950 = Lewis, Bernard: 'An Apocalyptic Vision of Islamic History'. *Bulletin of the School of Oriental and African Studies* 13, 1950, 308–338.

Lewis 1974 = Lewis, Bernard: 'On That Day: A Jewish Apocalyptic Poem on the Arab Conquest'. In *Melanges d'Islamologie: volume dédié à la mémoire de Armand Abel*, Salmon, Pierre (ed.). Leiden: Brill 1974, 197–200.

Lieu 1986 = Lieu Samuel N. C. (ed.), *The Emperor Julian: Panegyric and Polemic. Claudius Mamertinus, John Chrysostom, Ephrem the Syrian.* (Translated texts for historians. Greek series, 1). Liverpool: Liverpool University Press 1986.

Life of Theodore of Sykeon = *Bios tou hosiou patros hēmōn Theodōrou Archimandritou Sykeōn/Vie de Théodore de Sykéôn.* (Subsidia hagiographica, 48). Festugière, A.-J. (ed. and transl.). 2 vols., Bruxelles: Soc. des Bollandistes 1970.

Linder 1979 = Linder, A.: 'Jerusalem between Jews and Christians in the Byzantine Period'. *Cathedra* 2, 1979, 109–119.

Linder 1987 = Linder A. (ed. and transl.): *The Jews in Roman Imperial Legislation.* Detroit, Mich.: Wayne State University Press; Jerusalem: Israel Academy of Sciences and Humanities, 1987.

Louth 2008 = Louth, Andrew: 'Byzantium Transformed (600-700)'. In: *The Cambridge History of the Byzantine Empire c. 500-1492.* Shepard, Jonathan (ed.). Cambridge: Cambridge University Press 2008, 221–251.

Louth 2008a = Louth, Andrew: 'Eastern Orthodox Eschatology'. In: *The Oxford Handbook of Eschatology.* (Oxford handbooks). Walls, J. L. (ed.), New York; Oxford: Oxford University Press 2008, 233–247.

Luttwak 2009 = Luttwak, Edward N.: *The Grand Strategy of the Byzantine Empire.* Cambridge, Mass.: Belknap Press of Harvard University Press, 2009.

Magdalino 1993 = Magdalino, Paul: 'The History of the Future and its Uses: Prophecy, Policy and Propaganda'. In: *The Making of Byzantine History. Studies Dedicated to Donald M. Nicol.* (Publications, Centre for Hellenic Studies, King's College London, 1). Beaton, R. – Roueché, C. (eds.). Aldershot: Variorum 1993, 3–35.

Magdalino 1994 = Magdalino, Paul: 'Introduction'. In: *New Constantines: The Rhythm of Imperial Renewal in Byzantium, 4th–13th Centuries.* (Publications: Society for the Promotion of Byzantine Studies, 2). Magdalino, Paul (ed.). Aldershot: Variorum 1994, 2–9.

Magen – Talgam 1990 = Magen, Y. – Talgam, R.: 'The Monastery of Martyrius at Ma`aleh Adummim (Khirbet el-Murassas) and its Mosaics'. In: *Christian Archaeology in the Holy Land, New Discoveries. Essays in Honour of Virgilio C. Corbo, OFM* (Studium Biblicum Franciscanum: Collectio Maior, 36). Bottini, C. G. – Di Segni, L. – Alliata, E. (eds.). Jerusalem: Franciscan Printing Press, 1990, 91–151.

Magen 1993 = Magen, Y.: 'The Monastery of St. Martyrius at Ma`ale Adummim'. In: *Ancient Churches Revealed.* Tsafrir, Yoram (ed.). Jerusalem: Israel Exploration Society 1993, 170–196.

Magness 1992 = Magness, Jodi: 'A Re-examination of the Archaeological Evidence for the Sassanian Persian Destruction of the Tyropoeon Valley'. *Bulletin of the American Schools of Oriental Research* 287, 1992, 67–74.

Magness 2005 = Magness, Jodi: Review of: Mazar, Eilat: *The Temple Mount Excavations in Jerusalem 1968-1978 Directed by Benjamin Mazar – Final Reports Volume II, the Byzantine and Early Islamic Periods* (Qedem 43), Jerusalem: Hebrew University of Jerusalem 2003. *Bulletin of the American Schools of Oriental Research* 337, 2005, 104–106.

Magness 2010 = Magness, Jodi: 'Archaeological Evidence for the Sasanid Persian Invasion of Jerusalem'. In: *City of David. Studies of Ancient Jerusalem. The Eleventh Annual Conference.* Jerusalem: Megalim: City of David Institute for Jerusalem Studies, 2010, 41–61.

Maeir 1994 = Maeir, A.: 'The Excavations at Mamilla, Jerusalem Phase I (1989)'. In: *Ancient Jerusalem Revealed.* Geva, Hillel (ed.). Jerusalem: Israel Exploration Society 1994, 299–306.

Maeir 2000 = Maeir, A.: 'Sassanica Varia Palaestiniensia: A Sassanian Seal from T. Istaba, Israel, and other Sassanian Objects from the Southern Levant'. *Iranica Antiqua* 35, 2000, 159–183.

Mango 1985 = Mango, Cyril: 'Deux etudes sur Byzance et la Perse sassanide'. *Travaux et Mémoires* 9, 1985, 91–118.

Mango 1990 = Mango, Cyril: *Byzantium: The Empire of New Rome.* London: Weidenfeld and Nicholson 1990.

Mango 1992 = Mango, Cyril: 'The Temple Mount: 614-638 AD'. In: *Bayt al-Maqdis: 'Abd al-Malik's Jerusalem* (Oxford Studies in Islamic Art, 9). Johns, Jeremy – Raby, Julian (eds.). Oxford: Oxford University Press 1992, 1–16.

Mare 1987 = Mare, W. Harold: *The Archaeology of the Jerusalem Area.* Grand Rapids, Mich.: Baker Book House 1987.

Marmorstein 1906 = Marmorstein, Arthur: 'Les signes du Messie'. *Revue des études juives* 52, 1906, 176–186.

Mayerson 1964 = Mayerson, Philip: 'The First Muslim Attacks on Southern Palestine (A.D. 633-634)'. *Transactions and Proceedings of the American Philological Association* 95, 1964, 155–199.

Mazar 2003 = Mazar, Eilat: *The Temple Mount Excavations in Jerusalem 1968-1978 Directed by Benjamin Mazar – Final Reports Volume II, the Byzantine and Early Islamic Periods* (Qedem 43), Jerusalem: Hebrew University of Jerusalem 2003.

McCormick 1986 = McCormick, Michael: *Eternal Victory: Triumphal Rulership in Late Antiquity, Byzantium and the Early Medieval West.* (Past and Present Publications). Cambridge: Cambridge University Press 1986.

McGinn 1975 = McGinn, Bernard: 'Apocalypticism in the Middle Ages: An Historiographical Sketch'. *Medieval Studies* 37, 1975, 252–286.

McGinn 1979 = McGinn, Bernard: *Visions of the End: Apocalyptic Traditions in the Middle Ages*. New York: Columbia University Press 1979. Repr. 1998.

McGinn 1994 = McGinn, Bernard: *Antichrist: Two Thousand Years of the Human Fascination with Evil.* San Francisco, CA: HarperSanFrancisco 1994. Repr. New York: Columbia University Press 2000.

McGuckin 2006 = McGuckin, John 'Non-Violence and Peace Traditions in Early and Eastern Christianity'. In: *Religion, Terrorism and Globalisation: Non-Violence – A New Agenda.* Kuriakose, K. (ed.). New York: Nova Science Publishers, pp. 189–202.

Michael the Syrian *Chronique* = *Chronique de Michel le Syrien, patriarche jacobite d'Antioche (1166-1199).* Chabot, Jean-Baptiste (ed.). 4 vols., Paris: Leroux 1899–1910.

Milik 1961 = Milik, J. T.: 'La topographie de Jerusalem vers la fin de l'epoque Byzantine'. *Melanges de l'Université Saint Joseph* 37, Beirut 1961, 127–189.

Millar 1992 = Millar, F.: 'The Jews of the Graeco-Roman Diaspora Between Paganism and Christianity, AD 312–438'. In: *The Jews Among Pagans and Christians in the Roman Empire.* Lieu, J. – North, J. – Rajek, T. (eds.). London; New York: Routledge 1992, 97–124.

Millar 2004 = Millar, F.: 'Christian Emperors, Christian Church and the Jews of the Diaspora in the Greek East, CE 379–450'. *Journal of Jewish Studies* 55, 2004, 1–24.

Miller 1995 = Miller, Timothy S.: 'Introduction.' In: Miller – Nesbit (eds.) 1995: 1–17.

Miller – Nesbit (eds.) 1995 = Miller, Timothy S. – Nesbit, John (eds.): *Peace and War in Byzantium. Essays in Honor of George T. Dennis*. Washington, D.C.: The Catholic University of America Press 1995.

Mitchell 2007 = Mitchell, Stephen: *A History of the Later Roman Empire, AD 284-641: the Transformation of the Ancient World.* MA & Oxford: Blackwell 2007.

Morrison 2004 = Morrison, Craig E.: 'The Reception of the Book of Daniel in Aphrahat's Fifth Demonstration, "On Wars"'. *Hugoye: Journal of Syriac Studies* 7/1, 2004, 1–33.

Naggar 2002 = Naggar, Y.: 'Human Skeletal Remains from the Mamilla Cave, Jerusalem'. *`Atiqot* 43, 2002, 141–148.

Negev 1993 = Negev, A.: 'Eboda'. In: *New Encyclopedia of Archaeological Excavations in the Holy Land,* vol. 3. Stern, E. A. –Gilboa, A. (eds.). Jerusalem: Israel Exploration Society & Carta 1992, 1155–1165.

Nikephoros, *Breviarum Historicum* = *Breviarum Historicum, Short History*. (Dumbarton Oaks texts, 10; Corpus fontium historiae Byzantinae. Series

Washingtoniensis, 13). Mango, Cyril (ed. and transl.). Washington, D. C.: Dumbarton Oaks, Research Library and Collection 1990.

Oikonomidès 1971 = Oikonomidès, Nicholas: 'Correspondence between Heraclius and Kavādh-Široe in the Paschal Chronicle (628)'. *Byzantion* 41, 1971, 269–281.

Oikonomidès 1975 = Oikonomidès, Nicholas: 'A Chronological Note on the First Persian Campaign of Heraclius (622)'. *Byzantine and Modern Greek Studies* 1, 1975, 1–9.

Oikonomidès 1995 = Oikonomidès, Nicholas: 'The Concept of "Holy War" and Two Tenth-century Byzantine Ivories'. In: Miller – Nesbit (eds.) 1995: 62–87.

Olster 1991 = Olster, David Martin: 'The Date of George of Pisidia's "Hexaemeron"'. *Dumbarton Oaks Papers* 45, 1991, 159–172.

Olster 1994 = Olster, David Martin: *Roman Defeat, Christian Response and the Literary Construction of the Jew*. (Middle Ages series). Philadelphia: University of Pennsylvania Press 1994.

Olster 1998 = Olster, David Martin: 'Byzantine Apocalypses'. In: *The Encyclopedia of Apocalypticism*, Vol. 2, *Apocalypticism in Western History and Culture*, Collins, John J. – McGinn, Bernard – Stein, Stephen J. (eds.). New York and London: Continuum 1998, 48–73.

Olster 2006 = Olster, David Martin: 'Ideological Transformation and the Evolution of Imperial Presentation in the Wake of Islam's Victory'. In: *The Encounter of Eastern Christianity with Early Islam*. (The History of Christian-Muslim relations, 5). Grypeou, Emmanouela – Swanson, Mark N. – Thomas, David (eds.). Leiden; Boston: Brill 2006, 45–71.

Orfali 1924 = Orfali, Gaudence: *Gethsemani.* Paris: A. Picard 1924.

Orselli 1993 = Orselli, Alba Maria: *Santità militare e culto dei santi militari nell'impero dei romani (secoli VI-X)*. Bologna: *Lo* Scarabeo, 1993.

Ostrogorsky 1957 = Ostrogorsky, George: *History of the Byzantine State*, Hussey, Joan (transl.). New Brunswick, N.J.: Rutgers University Press 1957.

Ovadiah 1970 = Ovadiah, Asher: *Corpus of the Byzantine Churches in the Holy Land.* (Theophaneia: Beiträge zur Religions- und Kirchengeschichte des Altertums, 22). Kirson, Rose (transl.). Bonn: P. Hanstein, 1970.

Palmer – Brock – Hoyland 1993 = Palmer, Andrew N. (with Brock, Sebastian P. – Hoyland, Robert G.): *The Seventh Century in the West-Syrian Chronicles* (Translated Texts for Historians, 15). Liverpool: Liverpool University Press 1993.

Panaino 2004 = Panaino, Antonio: 'La Chiesa di Persia e l'Impero Sasanide. Conflitto e Integrazione'. In: *Cristianità d'Occidente e Cristianità d'Oriente* (Secoli VI-XI). (Settimane di studio del Centro Italiano di Studi sull'Alto medioevo, 51). Spoleto: Centro Italiano di Studi sull'Alto medioevo 2004, vol. 2, 765–863.

Panaino 2010 = Panaino, Antonio: 'The "Persian" Identity in Religious Controversies. Again on the Case of the "Divided Loyalty" in Sasanian Iran'. In *Iranian Identity in the Course of History. Proceedings of the Conference Held in Rome, 21–24 September 2005* (Serie Orientale Roma, 9). Cereti, Carlo G (ed.), with the assistance of Chiara Barbati, Matteo De Chiara and Gianfilippo Terribili. Roma: Istituto Italiano per l'Africa e l'Oriente, 2010, 227–241.

Patrich 1995 = Patrich, J.: 'Church, State and the Transformation of Palestine – the Byzantine Period (324–640 CE)'. In: *Archaeology of Society in the Holy Land.* Levy, Thomas E. (ed.). London: Leicester University Press 1995, 470–87.

Pertusi 1971 = Pertusi, Agostino: 'La Persia nelle fonti bizantine del secolo VII'. In: *Atti del Convegno internazionale sul tema: La Persia nel Medioevo, Roma, 31 marzo–5 aprile 1970.* (Accademia Nazionale dei Lincei. Problemi attuali di scienza e di cultura, quaderno, n. 160). Roma: Accademia Nazionale dei Lincei 1971, 605–628.

Peeters 1951 = Peeters, Paul: 'La prise de Jérusalem par les Perses'. In: Peeters, Paul: *Recherches d'histoire et de philologie orientales.* (Subsidia hagiographica, 27). I, Bruxelles: Société des Bollandistes 1951, 78–116.

Περὶ Στρατηγικῆς = "The Anonymous Byzantine Treatise on Strategy". In: Dennis, George T. (ed. and transl.): *Three Byzantine Military Treatises.* (Dumbarton Oaks texts, 9; Corpus fontium historiae Byzantinae, 25; Series Washingtonensis). Washington, D. C.: Dumbarton Oaks, Research Library and Collection 1985, 10–137.

Pernice 1905 = Pernice A.: *L'imperatore Eraclio. Saggio di storia bizantina.* Florence 1905.

Peters 1983 = Peters, Francis E.: 'Who Built the Dome of the Rock?'. *Graeco-Arabica* 1, 1983, 119–138.

Peters 1985 = Peters, Francis E.: *Jerusalem. The Holy City in the Eyes of Chroniclers, Pilgrims, and Prophets from the Days of Abraham to the Beginning of Modern Times*. Princeton, N.J.: Princeton University Press 1985.

Peters 1986 = Peters, Francis E.: *Jerusalem and Mecca. The Typology of the Holy City in the Near East.* (New York University Studies in Near Eastern civilization, 11). New York: New York University Press.

Podskalsky 1972 = Podskalsky, Gerhard: *Byzantinische Reicheschatologie. Die Periodisierung der Weltgeschichte in den vier Grossreichen (Daniel 2 und 7) und dem tausendjährigen Friedensreiche (Apok. 20).* (Münchener Universitäts-Schriften. Reihe der Philosophischen Fakultät, 9). München: Fink 1972.

Podskalsky 1973 = Podskalsky, Gerhard: 'Marginalien zur byzantinischen Reichseschatologie'. *Byzantinische Zeitschrift* 66, 1973, 351–358.

Podskalsky 1984 = Podskalsky, Gerhard: 'Représentation du temps dans l'eschatologie impériale Byzantine'. In: *Temps chrétiene de la fin de l'antiquité au moyen âge, IIIe–XIIIe siècles.* (Colloques internationaux du Centre national de la recherche scientifique, 604). Paris: Editions du Centre national de la recherche scientifique 1984, 439–450.

Podskalsky 2004 = Podskalsky, Gerhard: 'Politische Theologie in Byzanz zwischen Reichseschatologie und Reichsideologie'. In: *Cristianità d'Occidente e Cristianità d'Oriente* (Secoli VI-XI). (Settimane di studio del Centro Italiano di Studi sull'Alto medioevo, 51). Spoleto: Centro Italiano di Studi sull'Alto medioevo 2004, vol. 2, 1421–1433.

Prayer of Shimon bar Yohai = *Prayer of Shimon bar Yohai.* Eisenstein, Judah David (ed.). *Ozar Midrashim: A Library of Two Hundred Minor Midrashim. Edited with Introduction and Notes*, 2 vols., 1, 2.551–555 New York: J. D. Esienstein 1915, 551–555. English transl. in: Reeves, John C.: *Trajectories in Near Eastern Apocalyptic: a Postrabbinic Jewish Apocalypse Reader*. (Resources for biblical study, 45). Atlanta: Society of Biblical Literature, 2005, 40–67.

Prausnitz – Avi-Yonah – Barag 1967 = Prausnitz, M. W. – Avi-Yonah, M. – Barag, D.: *Excavations at Shavei Zion: the Early Christian Church. Report of the Excavations Carried out by the Israel Department of Antiquities and Museums (in Cooperation with the Hebrew University of Jerusalem).* (Monografie di archeologia e d'arte, 2). Roma: Centro per le antichità e la storia dell'arte del Vicino Oriente 1967.

Prawer 1996 = Prawer, Joshua: 'Christian Attitudes Towards Jerusalem in the Early Middle Ages'. In: Prawer – Ben-Shammai (eds.) 1996: 311–349.

Prawer – Ben-Shammai (eds.) 1996 = Prawer, Joshua – Ben-Shammai, Haggai (eds.): *The History of Jerusalem: the Early Muslim Period, 638–1099*. Jerusalem: Yad Izhak Ben-Zvi; New York: New York University Press 1996.

Prete 1966 = Prete, Serafino: *Escatologia e parenesi negli scrittori cristiani latini.* (Studi e ricerche, n.s., v. 15). Bologna: Università degli Studi di Bologna, Facoltà di Lettere e Filosofia 1966.

Pugliese Caratelli 1971 = Pugliese Caratelli, G.: 'La Persia dei Sasanidi nella storiografia romana da Ammiano a Procopio'. In: *Atti del Convegno internazionale sul tema: La Persia nel Medioevo, Roma, 31 marzo–5 aprile 1970.* (Accademia Nazionale dei Lincei. Problemi attuali di scienza e di cultura, quaderno 160). Roma: Accademia Nazionale dei Lincei 1971, 597–603.

Rabello 1987–88 = Rabello, Alfredo Mordechai: *Giustiniano, Ebrei e Samaritani alla luce delle fonti storico-letterarie e giuridiche.* (Monografie del Vocabolario di Giustiniano, 1-2). 2 vols., Milan: A. Giuffrè 1987–1988.

Reeves 2005 = Reeves, John C.: *Trajectories in Near Eastern Apocalyptic: a Postrabbinic Jewish Apocalypse Reader*. (Resources for biblical study, 45). Atlanta: Society of Biblical Literature, 2005.

Reich 1994 = Reich, R.: 'The Ancient Burial Ground in the Mamila Neighbourhood, Jerusalem'. In: *Ancient Jerusalem Revealed.* Geva, Hillel (ed.). Jerusalem: Israel Exploration Society 1994, 111–118.

Reich 1996 = Reich, R.: '"God Knows their Names" – Mass Christian Grave Revealed in Jerusalem'. *Biblical Archaeology Review* 22/2, 1996, 26–35.

Reinink 1985 = Reinink, Gerrit J.: 'Die Entstehung der syrischen Alexanderlegende als politisch-religiöse Propagandaschrift für Herakleios' Kirchenpolitik'. In: *After Chalcedon: Studies in Theology and Church History Offered to Professor Albert van Roey for his Seventieth Birthday.* (Orientalia Lovaniensia analecta, 18). Laga, Carl – Munitiz, Joseph – Van Rompay, Lucas (eds.). Leuven: Peeters, 263–281. Repr. in: Reinink 2005, III.

Reinink 2002 = Reinink, Gerrit J.: 'Heraclius, the New Alexander. Apocalyptic Prophecies during the Reign of Heraclius'. In: Reinink – Stolte (eds.) 2002: 81–95.

Reinink 2003 = Reinink, Gerrit J.: 'Alexander the Great in Seventh-Century Syriac 'Apocalyptic' Texts'. *Byzantinorossica* 2, 2003, 150–178; Repr. in: Reinink 2005, VI.

Reinink – Stolte (eds.) 2002 = Reinink, Gerrit J. – Stolte, Bernard H. (eds.): *The Reign of Heraclius (610–641): Crisis and* Confrontation. (Groningen studies in cultural change, 2). Leuven: Peeters 2002

Ribak 2007 = Ribak, Eliya: *Religious Communities in Byzantine Palestina. The Relationship between Judaism, Christianity and Islam, AD 400–700.* (BAR international series, 1646). Oxford: Archaeopress 2007.

Richardson – Granskou 1986 = Richardson, Peter – Granskou, David (eds.): *Anti-Judaism in Early Christianity*. (Studies in Christianity and Judaism = Etudes sur le christianisme et le judaïsme, 2–3). Waterloo, Ont.: Wilfrid Laurier University Press 1986, 2 vols.

Rubin 1998 = Rubin, Zeev: 'The Roman Empire in the 'Res Gestae Divi Saporis' – the Mediterranean World in Sasanian Propaganda'. In: *Ancient Iran and the Mediterranean World. Proceedings of an International Conference in Honour of Professor Jozef Wolski, held at the Jagiellonian University, Cracow, in September 1996.* (Electrum: studia z historii starożytnej = Studies in Ancient History, 2). Dąbrowa, E. (ed.). Kraków: Jagiellonian University Press 1998, 177–185.

Russell 2001 = Russell, James: 'The Persian Invasions of Syria/Palestine and Asia Minor in the Reign of Heraclius: Archaeological and Numismatic Evidence'. In: *Hoi skoteinoi aiōnes tou Byzantiou (7os – 9os ai.) / The Dark Centuries of Byzantium (7th–9^{th}c.).* (Diethnē symposia / Ethniko Hidryma Ereunōn, Institouto Byzantinōn Ereunōn, 9). Kountoura-Galakē, Eleōnora (ed.). Athens: Ethniko Hidryma Ereunōn, Institouto Byzantinōn Ereunōn 2001, 41–71.

Sako 1986 = Sako, L.: *Le rôle de la hiérarchie syriaque orientale dans les rapports diplomatiques entre la Perse et Byzance aux Ve – VIIe siècles.* Paris 1986.

Schäfer 1983 = Schäfer, Peter: *Geschichte der Juden in der Antike. Die Juden Palästinas von Alexander dem Großen bis zur arabischen Eroberung,* Stuttgart: Verlag Katholisches Bibelwerk; Neukirchen: Neukirchener Verlag 1983.

Sebeos = *Patmut'iwn Sebeosi,* Abgarian, Gevorg Varagi (ed.). Erevan: Haykakan SSH Gitut'yunneri Akademiayi Hratarakch'ut'yun, 1979. English translation: *The Armenian History Attributed to Sebeos*. (Translated Texts for Historians, 31). Thomson, Robert W. (transl.) – Howard-Johnston, James (hist. comm.) – Greenwood, Tim (assist.). Liverpool: Liverpool University Press 1999.

Schick 1995 = Schick, Robert: *The Christian Communities of Palestine in the Early Islamic Period. A Historical and Archaeological Study.* (Studies in Late Antiquity and Early Islam, 2). Princeton, N.J.: Darwin Press 1995.

Schick 2007 = Schick, Robert: 'Jerusalem in the Byzantine Period'. In: *Jerusalem before Islam.* (BAR international series, 1699). Kafafi, Zeidan – Schick, Robert (eds.). Oxford: British Archaeological Reports / Archaeopress 2007, 169–188.

Schippmann 1990 = Schippmann, Klaus: *Grundzüge der Geschichte des sasanidischen Reiches*. Darmstadt: Wissenschaftliche Buchgesellschaft, 1990.

Schlumberger 1890 = Schlumberger, Gustave: *Un empereur byzantin au dixième siècle: Nicéphore Phocas*, Paris: Firmin-Didot et cie 1890.

Schlumberger 1896–1905 = Schlumberger, Gustave: *L'épopée byzantine à la fin du dixième siècle: guerres contre les Russes, les Arabes, les Allemands, les Bulgares; luttes civiles contre les deux Bardas. Jean Tzimiscès. Les jeunes années de Basile II, le tueur de Bulgares (969–989*), 3 vols., Paris: Hachette & cie 1896–1905.

Schmidt 2002 = Schmidt, Katrin: *Friede durch Vertrag. Der Friedensvertrag von Kadesch von 1270 v. Chr., der Friede des Antalkidas von 386 v. Chr. und der Friedensvertrag zwischen Byzanz und Persien von 562 v. Chr.* Frankfurt am Main: Lang 2002.

Schneider 2006 = Schneider, Rolf Michael: 'Orientalism in Late Antiquity? The Oriental in Imperial and Christian Imagery'. In: Huyse – Wiesehöfer (eds.) 2006: 241–279.

Scott 1985 = Scott Roger D.: 'Malalas, The Secret History, and Justinian's Propaganda'. *Dumbarton Oaks Papers* 39, 1985, 99–109.

Shahbazi 2001 = Shahbazi, A. Shapur: 'Early Sasanians' Claim to Achaemenid Heritage'. *Nāme-ye Irān-e Bāstān, The International Journal of Ancient Iranian Studies* 1/1, 2001, 61–73.

Shahîd 1972 = Shahîd, Irfan: 'The Iranian Factor in Byzantium during the Reign of Heraclius'. *Dumbarton Oak Papers* 26, 1972, 295–320.

Shahîd 2004 = Shahîd, Irfan: 'The Last Sasanid-Byzantine Conflict in the Seventh Century: the Causes of its Outbreak.' In: *Atti del Convegno internazionale sul tema La Persia e Bisanzio. Accademia Nazionale dei Lincei, Roma, 14–18 ottobre 2002.* (Atti dei Convegni Lincei, 201). Gnoli, Gherardo (ed.). Rome: Accademia Nazionale dei Lincei 2004, 223–244.

Sharf 1955 = Sharf, Andrew: 'Byzantine Jewry in the Seventh Century'. *Byzantinische Zeitschrift* 48, 1955, 103-115. Repr. in: Sharf, Andrew: *Jews and Other Minorities in Byzantium*. Ramat-Gan: Bar-Ilan University Press, 1995, 96–109.

Sharf 1971 = Sharf, Andrew: *Byzantine Jewry from Justinian to the Fourth Crusade*. London: Routledge & K. Paul 1971.

Silberman 2001 = Silberman, Neil A.: 'Thundering Hordes: The Image of the Persian and Muslim Conquests in Palestinian Archaeology'. In: *Studies in the Archaeology of Israel and Neighboring Lands: in Memory of Douglas L. Esse*. (Studies in ancient oriental civilization, Oriental Institute of the University of Chicago, 59; Asor Books/American Schools of Oriental Research, 5). Wolff, Samuel R. (ed.). Chicago: Oriental Institute of the University of Chicago 2001.

Simon 1964 = Simon, M.: *Verus Israel: études sur les relations entre Chrétiens et Juifs dans l'empire romain (135–425)*. Paris: E. de Boccard 1964. 2e éd.

Smith 1996 = Smith Rowland B.: *Julian's Gods: Religion and Philosophy in the Thought and Action of Julian the Apostate*. London: Routledge 1996.

Sivan 2000 = Sivan, Hagith: 'From Byzantine to Persian Jerusalem: Jewish Perspectives and Jewish/Christian Polemics'. *Greek, Roman, and Byzantine Studies* 41, 2000, 277–306.

Sivan 2004 = Sivan, Hagith: 'Palestine between Byzantium and Persia (CE 614-18)'. In: *Atti del Convegno internazionale sul tema La Persia e Bisanzio. Accademia Nazionale dei Lincei, Roma, 14–18 ottobre 2002*. (Atti dei Convegni Lincei, 201). Gnoli, Gherardo (ed.). Rome: Accademia Nazionale dei Lincei 2004, 77–92.

Smith 1999 = Smith, R.: 'Telling tales. Ammianus' narrative of the Persian expedition of Julian'. In Drijvers, Jan W. – Hunt, David (eds.). *The Late Roman World and Its Historian: Interpreting Ammianus Marcellinus*. London: Routledge 1999, 89–104.

Sophronios, *Anacreontica* = *Sophronii Anacreontica* (Opuscula. Testi per esercitazioni accademiche, 10–12). Gigante, Marcello (ed.). Rome: Gismondi 1957.

Speck 1997 = Speck, Paul: 'The Apocalypse of Zerubavel and Christian Icons'. *Jewish Studies Quarterly* 4, 1997, 183–190.

Speck 1997a = Speck, Paul: 'Maximos der Bekenner und die Zwangstaufe durch Kaizer Herakleios'. In: Speck, Paul: *Beiträge zum Thema Byzantinische Feindseligkeit gegen die Juden im frühen siebten Jahrhundert* (Poikila Byzantina 15, Varia VI). Bonn: Habelt 1997, 441–467.

Speck 1997b = Speck, Paul: 'Die Predigt des Strategios'. In: Speck, Paul, *Beiträge zum Thema Byzantinische Feindseligkeit gegen die Juden im frühen siebten Jahrhundert*. (Poikila Byzantina 15, Varia VI). Bonn: Habelt 1997, 37–129.

Starr 1940 = Starr, Joshua: 'St Maximos and the Forced Baptism at Carthage'. *Byzantinisch-Neugriechische Jahrbücher* 16, 1940, 192–196.

Stemberger 1993 = Stemberger, Günter: 'Zwangstaufen von Juden im 4. bis 7. Jahrhundert. Mythos oder Wirklichkeit?'. In: *Judentum - Ausblicke und Einsichten. Festgabe für K. Schubert zum siebzigsten Geburtstag*. (Judentum und Umwelt, Realms of Judaism, 43). Maier, Johann – Stemberger, Günter – Thoma, Clemens (eds.). Frankfurt am Main: Lang 1993, 81–114.

Stemberger 1999 = Stemberger, Günter: 'Jerusalem in Early Seventh Century Aspirations of Christians and Jews'. In: Levine (ed.) 1999, 260–273.

Stemberger 2006 = Stemberger, Günter: 'Christians and Jews in Byzantine Palestine'. In: *Christians and Christianity in the Holy Land: from the Origins to the Latin Kingdoms*. (Cultural encounters in late antiquity and the Middle Ages, 5). Limor, Ora – Stroumsa, Gedaliahu A. G. (eds.). Turnhout: Brepols 2006, 293–321.

Stephenson 2007 = Stephenson, Paul, 'Imperial Christianity and Sacred War in Byzantium'. In: *Belief and Bloodshed: Religion and Violence across Time and Tradition*. Wellman, Jr., James K (ed.). Lanham; Boulder; New York; Toronto; Plymouth: Rowman & Littlefield 2007, 81–97.

Stoyanov 2009 = Stoyanov, Yuri: 'Norms of War in Eastern Orthodox Christianity'. In: *World Religions and Norms of War.* Popovski, V. – Reichberg, G. – Turner, N. (eds.). Tokyo; New York; Paris: United Nations University Press 2009, 166–220.

Strategikon = *Mauricius: Arta militară.* Mihăescu, H. (ed. and transl.). (Scriptores Byzantini, 6). Bucharest: Editura Academiei Republicii Socialiste România, 1970.

= *Das Strategikon des Maurikios.* Dennis, George T. (ed.) Gamillscheg, Ernst (transl.). (Corpus fontium historiae Byzantinae, 17; Series Vindobonensis). Wien: Verlag der Österreichischen Akademie der Wissenschaften 1981.

Strategios, *La prise de Jérusalem* = *La prise de Jérusalem par les Perses en 614.* (Corpus scriptorum Christianorum Orientalium, 202-203, Corpus scriptorum Christianorum Orientalium. Scriptores Iberici, 11-12). Garitte, Gérard (ed. and transl.). 2 vols. Louvain: Secrétariat du Corpus SCO 1960.

Strategios, *Expugnatio Hierosolymae* = *Expugnationis Hierosolymae AD 614 Recensiones Arabicae.* (Corpus scriptorum Christianorum orientalium, 347–348). Garitte, Gérard (ed. and transl.). 2 vols. Louvain: Secrétariat du Corpus SCO 1973–1974.

Stratos 1968 = Stratos, Andreas N.: *Byzantium in the Seventh Century,* I: *602–634.* Amsterdam: Hakkert 1968.

Stratos 1979 = Stratos, Andreas N.: 'La première campagne de l'Empereur Héraclius contre les Perses'. *Jahrbuch der Österreichischen Byzantinistik* 28, 1979, 63–74. Repr. in Stratos, Andreas N.: *Studies in 7th Century Byzantine Political History.* VI. London: Variorum 1983.

Stroumsa 2008 = Stroumsa, Gedaliahu A. G.: 'False Prophet, False Messiah and the Religious Scene in Seventh-Century Jerusalem'. In: *Redemption and Resistance: the Messianic Hopes of Jews and Christians in Antiquity,* Bockmuehl, Markus –Paget, James C. (eds.). London: T. & T. Clark 2008, 285–296.

Stroumsa – Limor 1996 = Stroumsa, Gedaliahu A. G. – Limor, Ora (eds.): *Contra Iudaeos: Ancient and Medieval Polemics between Christians and Jews.* (Texts and studies in medieval and early modern Judaism, 10). Tübingen: Mohr 1996.

Suolahti 1947 = Suolahti, J.: 'On the Persian Sources Used by the Byzantine Historian Agathias'. *Studia Orientalia* 13, 1947, 1–13.

Swift 1983 = Swift, Louis J: *Early Fathers on War and Military Service.* (Message of the Fathers of the Church, 19). Wilmington, Del.: Michael Glazier 1983.

Syntagma = *Syntagma Ton Theion kai Ieron Kanonon,* Ralles, Georgios A. – Potles, Michael (eds.). Athens: G. Chartophylax 1852.

Syriac Alexander Legend = *Syriac Alexander Legend.* Budge, Edgar A. W. (ed. and transl.). *The History of Alexander the Great: Being the Syriac Version of the Pseudo Callisthenes.* Cambridge: The University Press 1889, 255–275 (text), 144–158 (translation). Repr. Piscataway, N.J.: Gorgias Press, 2003.

Taylor 1993 = Taylor, Joan E.: *Christians and the Holy Places: The Myth of Jewish-Christian Origins*. Oxford: Clarendon Press 1993.

Taylor 1995 = Taylor, Miriam S.: *Anti-Judaism and Early Christian Identity: a Critique of the Scholarly Consensus*. (Studia post-biblica, 46). Leiden 1995.

Teitler 1999 = Teitler, H.: 'Viva vel lecta? Ammianus on Persia and the Persians'. In: Drijvers, Jan W. – Hunt, David (eds.). *The Late Roman World and its Historian: Interpreting Ammianus Marcellinus*. London: Routledge 1999, 216–223.

Theophanes *Chronographia* = *Theophanis Chronographia*. Boor, Carl de (ed.). 2 vols., Leipzig: Teubner 1883–1885. English translation: *The Chronicle of Theophanes Confessor: Byzantine and Near Eastern History, AD 284–813*. Mango, Cyril – Scott, Roger (transl.). Oxford: Clarendon Press 1997.

Theophylact Simocatta, *History* = *Theophylacti Simocattae Historiae*. Boor, Carl de (ed.). (Bibliotheca scriptorum Graecorum et Romanorum Teubneriana). Leipzig: Teubner 1887.

Thomson 1999 = Thomson, Robert W.: 'Biblical Themes in the Armenian Historian Sebēos'. In: *After Bardaisan: Studies on Continuity and Change in Syriac Christianity in Honour of Professor Han J. W. Drijvers*. (Orientalia Lovaniensia analecta, 89). Reinink, Gerrit J. – Klugkist, A. C. (eds.). Leuven: Peeters 1999, 295–303.

Thomson 2004 = Thomson, Robert W.: 'Armenian Ideology and the Persians'. In: *Atti del Convegno internazionale sul tema La Persia e Bisanzio. Accademia Nazionale dei Lincei, Roma, 14–18 ottobre 2002*. (Atti dei Convegni Lincei 201). Gnoli, Gherardo (ed.). Roma: Accademia Nazionale dei Lincei 2004, 373–390.

Thomson – Howard-Johnston – Greenwood 1999 = Thomson, Robert W. (transl.) – Howard-Johnston, James (hist. comm.) – Greenwood, Tim (assist.): *The Armenian History Attributed to Sebeos*. (Translated texts for historians, 31). 2 vols. Liverpool: Liverpool University Press 1999.

Treadgold 2001 = Treadgold, Warren T.: *A Concise History of Byzantium*, Basingstoke: Palgrave 2001.

Tsafrir 1999 = Tsafrir, Y.: 'Byzantine Jerusalem: The Configuration of a Christian City'. In: Levine (ed.) 1999: 133–151.

Tsafrir – Foerster 1997 = Tsafrir, Y. – Foerster, G.: 'Urbanism at Scythopolis – Bet-Shean in the Fourth to Seventh Centuries'. *Dumbarton Oaks Papers* 51, 1997, 85–146.

Tyerman 2006 = Tyerman, Christopher: *God's War: a New History of the Crusades*, London: Allen Lane 2006.

Tzaferis 1975 = Tzaferis, Vassilios: 'The Archaeological Excavation at Shepherd's Hill'. *Liber Annuus* 25, 1975, 5–52.

Van Bekkum 1993 = Van Bekkum, Wout J.: 'Anti-Christian Polemics in Hebrew Liturgical Poetry (Piyyut) of the Sixth and Seventh Centuries'. In: *Early Christian Poetry: A Collection of Essays*. (Supplements to Vigiliae Christianae, 22). Boeft, J. Den – Hilhorst, A. (eds.). Leiden: Brill 1993, 297–308.

Van Bekkum 2002 = Van Bekkum, Wout J.: 'Jewish Messianic Expectations in the Age of Heraclius'. In: Reinink – Stolte (eds.) 2002: 95–113.

Vasiliev 1952 = Vasiliev, Alexander A.: *History of the Byzantine Empire, 324–1453*. Oxford: Basil Blackwell 1952 (2nd English rev. ed.).

Verosta 1965 = Verosta, S.: 'Die oströmisch-persischen Verträge von 562 n. Chr. und ihre Bedeutung für das Völkerrecht'. *Anzeiger der Österreichischen Akademie der Wissenschaften in Wien. Philologisch-historische Klasse* 102, 1965, 153–156.

Vieillefond 1935 = Vieillefond, J.-R.: 'Les pratiques religieuses dans l'armée byzantine d'après les traités militaires'. *Revue des études anciennes* 37, 1935, 322–330.

Viscuso 1995 = Viscuso, Patrick: 'Christian Participation in Warfare: A Byzantine View'. In: Miller – Nesbit (eds.) 1995: 33–41.

Vita Constantini = *Vita Constantini*, In: *Kliment Okhridski. Sŭbrani sŭchineniia*, Angelov, B. S. – Kodov, Khr. (eds.). Sofia: Izdatelstvo na Bŭlgarskata Akademiia na Naukite 1973, 3, 89–109.

Walker 1990 = Walker, Peter W. L.: *Holy City, Holy Places? Christian Attitudes to Jerusalem and the Holy Land in the Fourth Century.* (Oxford Early Christian Studies). Oxford: Clarendon Press, 1990.

Watt 2002 = Watt, John W.: 'The Portrayal of Heraclius in Syriac Historical Sources'. In: Reinink – Stolte (eds.) 2002: 63–81.

Webster 1980 = Webster, Alexander F. C., 'Varieties of Christian Military Saints: From Martyrs under Caesar to Warrior Princes'. *St Vladimir's Theological Quarterly* 24, 1980, 3–35.

Weksler-Bdolah 2006-2007 = Weksler-Bdolah, S.: 'The Fortifications of Jerusalem in the Byzantine Period'. *Aram* 18–19, 2006–2007, 85–112.

Wheeler 1991 = Wheeler, Brannon M.: 'Imagining the Sasanian Capture of Jerusalem. The "Prophecy and Dream of Zerubbabel" and Antiochus Strategios' "Capture of Jerusalem"'. *Orientalia Christiana Periodica* 57, 1991, 69–85.

Whitby 1994 = Whitby, Mary: 'A New Image for a New Age: George of Pisidia on the Emperor Heraclius'. In: *The Roman and Byzantine Army in the East*, Dąbrowa, E. (ed.). Kraków: Uniwersytet Jagielloński, Instytut Historii 1994, 197–225.

Whitby 1998 = Whitby, Mary: 'Defender of the Cross: George of Pisidia on Emperor Heraclius and His Deputies'. In: *The Propaganda of Power. The Role of Panegyric in Late Antiquity.* (Mnemosyne, Bibliotheca Classica Batava. Supplementum, 183). Whitby, Mary (ed.). Leiden: Brill 1998, 247–273.

Whitby 2002 = Whitby, Mary: 'George of Pisidia's Presentation of the Reign of Heraclius and his Campaigns: Variety and Development'. In: Reinink – Stolte (eds.) 2002: 157–173.

Whitby 1988 = Whitby, Michael: *The Emperor Maurice and his Historian: Theophylact Simocatta on Persian and Balkan Warfare* (Oxford Historical Monographs). Oxford: Clarendon Press; New York: Oxford University Press, 1988.

Whitby 1992 = Whitby, Michael: 'Greek Historical Writing after Procopius: Variety and Validity'. In: *The Byzantine and Early Islamic Near East* I: *Problems in the Literary Source Material*. (Studies in Late Antiquity and Early Islam, 1). Cameron, Averil – Conrad, Lawrence I. (eds.). Princeton, N.J.: Darwin Press 1992, 25–81.

Whitby 1998 = Whitby, Michael: 'Deus Nobiscum: Christianity, Warfare, and Morale in Late Antiquity'. In: *Modus Operandi: Essays in Honour of Geoffrey Rickman*. (Bulletin of the Institute of Classical Studies. Supplement, 71). Austin, M. – Harries, J. – Smith, C. (eds.). London: Institute of Classical Studies, School of Advanced Study, University of London 1998, 191–208.

Whitby 2002a = Whitby, Michael: *Rome at War AD 293–696*. (Essential histories). Oxford: Osprey 2002.

Whitby – Whitby (transl.) 1986 = Whitby, Mary – Whitby, Michael (transl.): *The History of Theophylact Simocatta*. Oxford: Clarendon Press; New York: Oxford University Press 1986.

Whittow 1996 = Whittow, Mark: *The Making of Orthodox Byzantium 600–1025*. Berkeley: University of California Press 1996.

Wiesehöfer 1994 = Wiesehöfer, Josef: *Das antike Persien. Von 550 v. Chr. bis 650 n. Chr.* Zürich: Artemis; München: Winkler 1994.

Wiesehöfer 2001 = Wiesehöfer, Josef: *Ancient Persia from 550 BC to 650 AD*. Azodi, A. (transl.). London: I.B. Tauris 2001.

Wiesehöfer 2005 = Wiesehöfer, Josef: *Iraniens, grecs et romains*. (Cahiers de Studia Iranica 32). Paris: Association pour l'avancement des études iraniennes 2005.

Wiesehöfer 2005a = Wiesehöfer, Josef: 'Rūm as enemy of Iran'. In: Gruen, Erich S. (ed.). *Cultural Borrowings and Ethnic Appropriations in Antiquity*. (Oriens et Occidens, 8) Stuttgart: Steiner 2005, 105–120.

Wiesehöfer 2006 = Wiesehöfer, Josef: 'Statt einer Einleitung: 'Randkultur' oder 'Nabel der Welt'? Das Sasanidenreich und der Westen. Anmerkungen eines Althistorikers'. In: Huyse – Wiesehöfer (eds.) 2006: 9–29.

Wilken 1971 = Wilken, Robert L.: *Judaism and the Early Christian Mind: a Study of Cyril of Alexandria's Exegesis and Theology*. New Haven: Yale University Press 1971.

Wilken 1983 = Wilken, Robert L.: *John Chrysostom and the Jews: Rhetoric and Reality in the Late 4th Century*. (The Transformation of the Classical Heritage, 4). Berkeley and Los Angeles: University of California Press, 1983.

Wilken 1985 = Wilken, Robert L.: 'The Restoration of Israel in Biblical Prophecy: Christian and Jewish Response in the Early Byzantine Period'. In: *'To See Ourselves as Others See Us': Christians, Jews and 'Others' in Late Antiquity*. (Scholars Press Studies in the Humanities). Nesner, Jacob – Frerichs, Ernest S. (eds.). Chico, CA: Scholars Press 1985, 443–471.

Wilken 1992 = Wilken, Robert L.: 1992. *The Land Called Holy. Palestine in Christian History and Thought*. New Haven: Yale University Press 1992.

Wilkinson 1977 = Wilkinson, John: *Jerusalem Pilgrims before the Crusades*, Warminster: Aris & Phillips 1977.

Williams 1935 = Williams, Arthur L.: *Adversus Judaeos: a Bird's-eye View of Christian Apologiae until the Renaissance*. Cambridge: University Press 1935.

Yahalom 1979 = Yahalom, Yosef: 'On the Validity of Literary Works as Historical Sources'. *Cathedra* 11, 1979, 125–133 (Hebrew).

Yahalom 1992 = Yahalom, Yosef: 'The Transition of Kingdoms in Eretz Israel as Conceived by Poets and Homilists'. *Shalem* 6, 1992, 1–22 (Hebrew).

Yahalom 1996 = Yahalom, Yosef: 'The Temple and the City in Liturgical Hebrew Poetry'. In: Prawer, Joshua – Ben-Shammai, Haggai (eds.): *The History of Jerusalem: the Early Muslim Period, 638–1099*. Jerusalem: Yad Izhak Ben-Zvi; New York: New York University Press 1996, 270–295.

Yarshater 1971 = Yarshater, Ehsan: 'Were the Sasanians Heirs to the Achaemenids?'. In: *Atti del Convegno internazionale sul tema: La Persia nel Medioevo, Roma, 31 marzo–5 aprile 1970.* (Accademia Nazionale dei Lincei. Problemi attuali di scienza e di cultura, quaderno 160). Roma: Accademia Nazionale dei Lincei 1971, 517–531.

Zuckerman 2002 = Zuckerman, Constantin: 'Heraclius in 625'. *Revue des études byzantines* 60, 2002, 189–197.